GOING HOME

GOING HOME

A Play in Two Acts

by Alan Plater

SQUARE ONE BOOKS LIMITED

GOING HOME
©Alan Plater 1990

First published in 1990 by
SQUARE ONE BOOKS LTD
5 St Thomas Road, Brentwood, Essex, CM14 4DB

ISBN 1 872747 01 9

Publisher and Designer: Colin Larkin
Editorial and Production Assistant: Susan Pipe
Editiorial Assistant: Aileen Tyler
Marketing: John Eley
Special thanks: Shirley Rubinstein and Tim Flood
For fast printing and binding:
Neil MacDonald and Colin Pooley
Cover photograph: Jonathan Keenan 061-226 0155

This book has been typeset in Monotype Ellington 10 point on 12.5
Inspired by the late Duke Ellington.

Produced on an Apple Macintosh IICX 4/80
using Quark Xpress 2.12 and Microsoft Word 4
Cover printing by Technique
Printed and bound in England by Biddles Ltd

Alan Plater

Alan Plater was born in Jarrow in 1935. Brought up and educated in Hull, he studied Architecture in Newcastle during the 1950's, but has been a full-time writer since 1961, with over 250 credits in radio, television, theatre and films - plus three novels and occasional journalism.

His first plays were written for radio, a medium he still loves. His play, *The Journal Of Vasilije Bogdanovic*, won the 1983 Sony Radio Award for the best drama script.

His television career started in the 1960's with a string of single plays and work on the pioneering *Z Cars* series. Since then his work has embraced plays and series, situation comedy, documentaries and dramatisations. *Barchester Chronicles*, from Trollope's novels, received a BAFTA nomination, as did *The Crystal Spirit*, a film about George Orwell.

In 1985 he won the Royal Television Society's Writer's Award for *The Biederbecke Affair*, *On Your Way Riley!* - a television version of his stage play first seen at the Theatre Royal, Stratford East, with Brian Murphy and Maureen Lipman, and *Edward Lear - At The Edge Of The Sand*.

The following year, *Coming Through*, a film about D.H. Lawrence, starring Kenneth Branagh, won major awards at festivals in New York and San Francisco.

More recent work includes, *The Beiderbecke Tapes*, *The Beiderbecke Connection*, *Fortunes Of War* - voted the Best Series by the Broadcasting Press Guild in 1988; and *A Very British Coup*, starring the late Ray McAnally, which won the BAFTA Best Series Award, the Broadcasting Press Guild, the Royal Television Society - plus an International Emmy (U.S.A.), the Golden Fleece of Georgia (U.S.S.R.)

and Best Series Award and Grand Prix at the Banff Television Festival (Canada).

In 1989 he won the coveted BAFTA Writer's Award, proving, he says, that if you buy enough tickets you end up winning the raffle.

On the big screen his career started in 1969 with *The Virgin And The Gypsy*, from D.H.Lawrence's novel, and has also included work with Richard Lester on *Juggernaut*, *Priest Of Love* starring Ian McKellen and Janet Suzman and *It Shouldn't Happen To A Vet*.

His work in the theatre includes *Close The Coalhouse Door*, a musical about the Durham miners, written with Alex Glasgow and Sid Chaplin, a key work in the development of British political theatre: two celebrated adaptations of Bill Tidy's *Fosdyke Saga*, *On Your Way Riley!*, *Prez* - a jazz opera about Lester Young, *In Blackberry Time* from Sid Chaplin's stories; *Rent Party*, a musical set in 1930's Harlem, again at the Theatre Royal, Stratford East. His most recent play is *Sweet Sorrow*, a comical and thought provoking play about Philip Larkin.

Plater is now firmly established as one of Britain's premier writers. His unassuming nature and laconic sense of humour have won him many friends and admirers.

In his spare(ish) time he indulges his passion for jazz, snooker, Hull City, the Writers' Guild of Great Britain, his grown-up children and his dog, 'The Duke', named after Ellington. He and his wife Shirley live, very contentedly, in North London.

Introduction

A distinguished colleague in the writing trade - from memory, Christopher Hampton - was once asked by a well-meaning journalist where plays came from. He replied that he wished he knew, so he could go back to the same place every time he needed one.

Going Home is, to some extent anyway, an exception to this rule. In 1987, I worked with Newcastle's Live Theatre company on a stage version of seven stories by the late Sid Chaplin, under the collective title, *In Blackberry Time*. I shared the writing with Sid's son, Michael, and it was a lovely adventure.

Those who know Sid's work will be familiar with the tough and tender simplicity running through it. His early stories were often based on yarns told to him by pitmen at the coal-face, and he never lost this clarity of meaning and intent. Obscurity was not his style and is, in any case, highly overrated as a literary device. Genuine simplicity is the real mark of sophistication, whether in a drawing by Picasso or a solo by Lester Young.

It was therefore a slight shock to the system when we came across a story called *Where Is My Old Friend Bing Crosby Tonight?* - a tale of a meeting down by the river, hung over with the sounds of popular music and old regrets, shadowed by the mean streets of the city. It's a mysterious and ambiguous piece in a style I defined, too cutely, as Chandler-on-Tyne.

The story wouldn't leave us alone and one evening Max Roberts, director of *In Blackberry Time*, said something along the lines of: 'Why don't you write a full-length play about a guy doing some investigation in and around Newcastle, with a tenor saxophone playing in the background?'

That was the start - the theatrical notion of a man telling his tale with cool music in the background and sometimes the foreground. Other elements then moved in, most of them biographical but that can't be helped: every writer's life is his alphabet. You listen to the stories at the coal-face and try to re-tell them in a way that decently honours the original.

The biographical elements that have breathed life into *Going Home* are, in edited highlight form: my childhood in Jarrow: the years in Newcastle as a student in the 1950's, and a wonderful four months spent in Australia in 1988, as Writer-in-Residence at the Film, Television and Radio School in Sydney. I am madly in love with Australia, along with Tyneside, football and jazz.

It was a short imaginative leap from these elements to the idea of a native Geordie, returning to Tyneside after thirty years in Australia - no longer a detective investigating a criminal misdemeanour, but just an ordinary guy asking the eternal questions: Who am I? How did I get here? And what am I going to do tomorrow?

Essentially it's a love story, but concerned with infinite varieties of love: our love of people and places, of music and culture (which naturally includes football, prominently displayed) and, much neglected in these times, love of work. In an age when apprenticeships have gradually been replaced by schemes, we need to think again about pride in things well made, and quickly, while there's still a little bit left. Theme parks, fast food joints, monetarism and muzak are no substitute. I hate them with an eager, all-consuming venom, though I'm sad for their victims.

The play has grown from investigative thriller into a personal quest, though I hope it's done so without sinking in a swamp of art and pretension. It remains a simple yarn about a guy going home except, of course, that such a tale can never be that simple, if only because of the ghosts in the back yard that can only be laid to rest by going down to the river and staring at the black water. Then, with a little luck, we might find a happy ending, or at least a happy beginning.

Alan Plater
11th September 1990

Northern Stage Company's production of
GOING HOME was first performed at the
Playhouse, Newcastle Upon-Tyne from
1st to 17th November 1990.

Directed by Max Roberts

Cast List

BOB	**Tim Healy**
MARY/	**Su Elliott**
LIZ	
RALPH	**David Whitaker**
FATHER/	**Colin Maclachlan**
HARRY/	
WAITER	
MOTHER/	**Denise Welch**
SHEILA	
KENNY	**Mike Elliott**

Other parts played by members of the company

Design: Nigel Hook
Lighting Design: Chris Jaeger

Music written and arranged by Ian Carr,
and played by

Trumpet:	**Ian Carr**
Saxes:	**Lewis Watson**
Piano:	**Paul Flush**
Drums:	**Adrian Tilbrook**
Acoustic Bass:	**Peter Ayton**

ACT ONE

A jazz quintet with tenor sax lead is playing BODY AND SOUL, in the Coleman Hawkins tradition.

Lights fade up slowly and gently to reveal the outline of a great bridge, dominating the stage, as it will throughout: Sydney Harbour Bridge or Tyne Bridge - it's the same shape. Only the size is different - and there's a world between them. Then we see the lights of Sydney, the water of the harbour and the white silhouette of the Opera House, shining like an exotic sea-shell.

And then we see BOB, a Geordie-in-exile, fifty years old, give or take a year.

BOB: The Sydney Harbour Bridge, New South Wales, Australia. Built in 1932. The locals call it the Coat Hanger. But...and this bit's important...before they built it, they built the Tyne Bridge as a sort of dummy run. I suppose the powers-that-be argued that if it was good enough for Newcastle and

Gateshead it would certainly be good
enough for a bunch of colonials here in the
outback. On the other hand, the powers-
that-be *might* have argued that if the thing
was a total disaster and collapsed at the
official opening, they might as well sacrifice
a few hundred Geordies, rather than proper
human beings. The powers-that-be tend
to think like that about Geordies.
(Maybe a half-smile.)
I'm not crazy about powers-that-be. Some
people think I'm prejudiced.
(He reacts to the music.)
Man, that's a good sound. You can hear
all sorts of music here on the harbour.
Yonder's the Opera House. You get all
sorts of music there. Schubert,
Stravinsky, Shirley Bassey. The theme
music from the World Cup. And up
there's The Rocks. That's the old part of
the city, a bit like the Quayside. It all
comes tumbling down to the water.
Different water, different bridge, a world
away, but it was the music that did it.
Definitely the music.
(He again ponders the music then:)

BOB: Not just the music, but that tune. Body
and Soul. I heard it and I said: Bobby
lad, they're playing your tune. Now I realise
that sounds like a lorry load of twenty-four
carat crap but it isn't. Well, not entirely.
See, on my last night in Newcastle, before I
fled the country, I mean *left* the
country...I'd heard some guy playing Body
and Soul on a tenor sax...it wasn't the last
thing that happened but it was the last

thing I remembered. And that was thirty years ago.

So that's how it happened. I'd been for supper at Doyle's. The best fish restaurant in Sydney. Overlooking the harbour. They sell oysters at **a** price a working man can afford. And I heard the music. Floating across the water, like it had come all the way from the Tyne. And I know it's crazy, man, but that's when I knew. It was time. Time for me to be going home.

(BODY AND SOUL ends.
The sound of an air liner in flight.
BOB crosses to a chair and sits down: not an airliner seat. Do it with acting, yes?)

BOB: I don't know whether you've ever flown from Australia to England. I'm not saying it would be quicker to walk. But it would *seem* quicker. They put you in a seat eighteen inches wide, between two other seats eighteen inches wide. On this side there's always an eighteen stone man who needs most of your seat.
(He mimes the arrival of the fat man.)
And on this side there's a woman, a new Aussie immigrant from Yugoslavia. She's dead keen to practise her English.
For twenty-six hours. She's on her way to Dubrovnik to collect her sewing machine. I *think* that's what she said.
(He turns to the fat man.)
Yes, I'm off back to Newcastle. I'll be there in time for United's first home game of the season.

(Reacts) Er...football. *(To audience)* Not only fat but he's a rugby union man.
(He turns to the Yugoslav woman, speaking slowly and precisely, as to the village idiot.)

BOB: I...am...go...ing...to...vis...it...my...sis...ter... and...her...hus...band...in...Heat...on...
(BOB puts on a headset.)
Then, to make it even more interesting, you get three inflight movies about little boys and dogs having extremely exciting adventures, seven channels of music all written by Andrew Lloyd Webber, and nine trays of plastic food.
(Tries to edge away from the fat man.)
Fatso spills most of his. Conclusion. Stevenson was wrong. To arrive is ten times better than to travel hopefully. He should have stuck to steam engines.

(Cut airliner sound.
BOB gets up, addressing each of his neighbours in turn.)
(To fat man) See you later, sport.
(To audience) All Australians say that. They hardly ever do it. *(To woman)* Good...bye...have...a...safe...on... ward...jour...ney...pet. *(To audience)* Trouble is, you end up *talking* like British Airways.

(Music: a little morsel of Lionel Hampton's FLYING HOME.
BOB crosses the stage, exits then re-enters immediately with luggage trolley bearing a large suitcase and a couple of duty-free bags.

His sister MARY and her husband RALPH
enter from the other side. They are
maybe five years younger than BOB.

Behind all this, the Sydney Harbour
Bridge becomes the Tyne Bridge and the
sky darkens.
BOB, MARY and RALPH meet centre
stage.)

BOB:	Mary pet!
MARY:	Bob!

(They embrace.
As they break away:)

MARY:	My brother Bob. My husband Ralph.

(The two men shake hands.)

RALPH:	Hi, Bob.
BOB:	G'day, Ralphy.
MARY:	Is that Australian? G'day?
BOB:	Yes. I'm bi-lingual. In two languages.

(They take the luggage from the trolley. BOB
points at it.)

BOB:	Look at that.
RALPH:	What?
BOB:	It says...Not to be removed from Bahrein Airport.
RALPH:	No it doesn't.
MARY:	*(To RALPH)* Sorry, love. Should have warned you. My brother has a sense of humour.

15

(They cross to a living/dining room area. Essentially it's a table set for a meal with optional trimmings. BOB takes a couple of bottles from the duty-free bag, and puts them on the table.)

BOB: There's your duty-free.
RALPH: Thanks, that's great.

(BOB opens the case and brings out six more bottles.)

BOB: And there's your duty-free.
RALPH: How much are you allowed?
BOB: I did a deal with a fat man and a woman from Dubrovnik.

*(Music finishes hereabouts.
MARY enters carrying supper tray.)*

MARY: Shift the bottles. I need space.

(The men do as instructed.)

BOB: Have you got glasses?
RALPH: No, I wear lenses.
BOB: Glasses for drinking out of, man.
RALPH: Oh. Sorry.

*(RALPH finds glasses.
MARY serves the food.
BOB pours drinks.
As he does so:)*

BOB: What's for supper like?
MARY: I tried to get fatted calf, but I was advised

	against it. It's got some sort of official disease.
BOB:	How do you know it's an official disease?
MARY:	The government says it's safe to eat.
BOB:	I was hoping there might be pease pudding.
RALPH:	We had the last tin at the weekend.
BOB:	Tin? Did you say tin?
RALPH:	Well, yes. Only 'cause it's the truth like.
BOB:	Do you not make your own pease pudding, our Mary?
MARY:	No, I do not. And they've dug up the tramlines, and pensioned off the old lamp-lighter. Any more questions?

(BOB hesitates then)

| BOB: | Not for the moment. |

(He hands round the glasses. They sit down at the table, glasses raised.)

RALPH:	Cheers.
MARY:	Cheers.
BOB:	Cheers.

(They start to eat)

BOB:	My mother made wonderful pease pudding.
MARY:	You're fifteen years too late.
BOB:	I realise.
MARY:	Is that the only reason you came home?
BOB:	What?
MARY:	Pease pudding?
BOB:	No.
MARY:	You could learn to make it yourself.
BOB:	Men's liberation? All that?
MARY:	Why not?

BOB:	I've lived with male chauvinists too long.
MARY:	That's your problem.

(RALPH looks from one to the other through all this, like an umpire at Wimbledon.)

RALPH:	Mary's right.
BOB:	About making my own?
RALPH:	She said you always used to argue.
BOB:	A good argument, keeps your brain alert.
MARY:	Is *that* why you came home? You needed an argument?
BOB:	I'll tell you. Every July, as we're coming out of winter...
RALPH:	You have winter in July?
BOB:	Yes. Summer's in January. So anyway, every July...
RALPH:	That's because you're on the other side of the world...
BOB:	I believe that has something to do with it. And we have North in the South and vice versa, and also the hands on the clock go anti-clockwise.
RALPH;	Is that right?
BOB:	So anyway, every July...
RALPH:	It can't be right.
MARY:	Oh for God's sake, man, just tell us what happens every July!
BOB:	What happens is I get this feeling...I've got to go home in time for United's first home game.
MARY:	You've come all this way just to go to a football match?
BOB:	Why not? I'm a Geordie.
RALPH:	I can understand that.

BOB:	See? Your husband understands. That proves it makes sense.
MARY:	It proves you're both men.
BOB:	So that's settled. Me and you'll go to the match on Saturday, all right, Ralphy lad?
RALPH:	Sorry, Bob. Can't do that.
BOB:	What do you mean, you can't do that? She doesn't make you go shoppping on a Saturday afternoon, does she? Or is that when you wash the car? Surely not. Sunday morning's the time to wash the car.

(MARY turns to RALPH.)

MARY:	Tell him.
BOB:	Tell me what? Is there a terrible family secret I don't know about?
MARY:	Tell him.
RALPH:	I'm a Sunderland supporter.

(There's a silence. Naturally.
Maybe a little bluesy comment from the band.
BOB turns to MARY.)

BOB:	You never told me you'd married a Sunderland supporter.
RALPH:	So obviously there's no way I can set foot inside St James's Park except if Sunderland's playing there.
BOB:	*(Grudgingly)* Yes. I can see that.
RALPH:	And that's not likely to happen for a bit with United in the Second Division. We got promoted to the First, like...
BOB:	*(Breaks in)* You didn't get promoted! You sneaked into the First Division on account of some clerical errors in Swindon. It wasn't promotion. It was a three-card trick.

19

RALPH:	We beat United in the play-offs, two legs, head to head, and I've got it on video if you want to see the evidence.
MARY:	Shut up! Both of you! *(They shut up. Both of them.* *Another bluesy comment, continuing* *through:)*

RALPH:	I'll clear away.
BOB:	I need a breath of fresh air.

(BOB crosses to a back yard area:
essentially an old wooden bench, in a
pool of light.
MARY follows him.
Music drifts on.)

MARY:	Is that fresh enough for you?
BOB:	Fresher than I remember it. What happened to all the smoke?
MARY:	It was abated. Officially.

(BOB touches the bench.)

BOB:	You've still got the old bench?
MARY:	We brought it over from Byker when my Mam died.
BOB:	Good.

(He sits down.
Music stops hereabouts.)

MARY:	Why did you come home?
BOB:	I told you. I want to see the match.
MARY:	Bollocks.
BOB:	Fair comment. Maybes I just wanted to sit on this bench and have a bit crack.

(MARY hesitates, then sits down with him.)

MARY:	Right. Go ahead.
BOB:	So. How's things?
MARY:	Fine.
BOB:	And what's happened these last thirty years?
MARY:	Not a lot really.
BOB:	Not a lot! Ye bugger, we're talking about nearly half a lifetime! Something must have happened.
MARY:	Well. You leave school. Get married. Have kids. Kids grow up, leave home. You stay married.
BOB:	This is your life.
MARY:	There's plenty worse lives.
BOB:	I daresay.
MARY:	And what happened to you?
BOB:	Emigrated. Got married. Had kids. Kids grew up and left home. Wife grew up and left home.
MARY:	You can say all that in letters and phone calls.
BOB:	We do. We did.

(A silence.)

MARY:	Why didn't you come home for Mam's funeral?
BOB:	That's fifteen years ago.
MARY:	I know when it was. I want to know why you didn't come home.
BOB:	She was dead.
MARY:	You go to funerals to help the living, not the dead.
BOB:	I know. I'm sorry. I wasn't up to the job. There were reasons.

MARY:	*(Finishing thought)* But your sister wouldn't understand...
BOB:	Not sure I understand myself.
MARY:	Oh God! I'm sitting next to a male menopause.
BOB:	How's what?
MARY:	Middle-aged man agonising over the meaning of his life.
BOB:	Is there a lot of that in Heaton?
MARY:	Quite a bit. There's more in Gosforth and I believe it peaks in Jesmond. But if that's all it is...a mid-life crisis...I'll not bother worrying about it.
BOB:	I started my mid-life crisis when I was fifteen. Kenny Turnbull explained girls to me. It's been going on ever since. Wonder if Kenny's still around? He'll go to the match with me. Do you know if he's still around?
MARY:	No idea.

(Another bluesy phrase drifts in).

BOB:	The last time I saw my Mam and Dad together, they were sitting on this bench. In the back yard.

(He turns to look across the stage.
In another pool of light, their MOTHER and
FATHER sit on an identical bench.
It is 1944. Both are dressed accordingly,
FATHER in army uniform: the Durham Light
Infantry to be precise.)

BOB:	It was 1944. He was home on leave.
FATHER:	Hey, young Bobby!
BOB:	Yes Dad.

FATHER:	You'll look after your mother while I'm away winning the war.
BOB:	Yes Dad.
FATHER:	Make sure she goes to the air raid shelter when the sirens go.
BOB:	Yes Dad.
FATHER:	Good lad.
BOB:	Are you going to kill lots of Germans?
FATHER:	Only if they try to kill me first.
MOTHER:	He's going to take great care of himself, aren't you?
FATHER:	I certainly will. *(To BOB.)* Atten...shun!

(BOB stands up to attention.)

FATHER: By the left...quick...march!

(Drummer provides martial backing.
Maybe the horn player adds the D.L.I.
music on clarinet/penny whistle/or such.
BOB marches across the stage.)

FATHER: About...turn!

(BOB does the about turn.
Then, abruptly, the music stops.
Lights out on MOTHER and FATHER.
BOB is left marching on his own.)

BOB: He taught me all the army drill. With a
broom handle for a rifle.
(Picks up a broom handle.)
Shoulder arms! Present arms! Stand at ease!
Stand easy...

(BOB goes through the routine then, on the final command, puts down the broom handle.)

MARY: Did he always make you march as fast as that?

BOB: He was in the Durham Light Infantry. They always marched fast. That's why they were called the Light Infantry.

MARY: Did he teach you anything else?

BOB: Yes. I know all about Hughie Gallacher and Billy McCracken. Learned it all sitting on this bench.

MARY: Don't tell me. Let me guess. Footballers?

BOB: Footballers.

MARY: I wish I'd known my Dad.

BOB: I wish that, too, pet.

*(They fall silent for a while.
A little night music then:)*

BOB: I didn't know I knew that.

MARY: No idea what you're talking about, kid.

BOB: I didn't know I still remembered the rifle drill.

MARY: It's a useful skill. Just make sure you always travel with a broom handle.

BOB: It's like...who won the F.A. Cup in 1932? Or...what was the Labour majority in the 1945 General Election...or name the tenor saxophone player on the legendary version of Body and Soul recorded on October 11th 1939...

(MARY ponders the questions.)

MARY: Don't know. I give in.

BOB:	Newcastle United, one hundred and forty-six and Coleman Hawkins.
MARY:	Fantastic. You've won a holiday for two in Whitley Bay.
BOB:	I've got nobody to go with.
MARY:	Whose fault's that?
BOB:	I plead guilty on all charges. But that's not the point.
MARY:	There's a point to all this?
BOB:	The point is, I know all those things, but I never sat down with a book and learned them. They're just there, in my bones, and I've no idea how they got there. It's like a sing-song. The piano starts up an old tune and we all join in and we know the words, even though we never learned them.
	(Pause.)
BOB:	Dreamtime.
MARY:	Huh?
BOB:	The Aboriginal people in Australia call it dreamtime.
	(He looks at her, checking she's on roughly the right wave-length.)
BOB:	You know about Aboriginal people?
MARY:	Certainly I do. They were there thousands of years ago, right?
BOB:	Right. Well done.
MARY:	I watch documentaries on BBC2. I know what's good for me.
BOB:	They have this thing called dreamtime. They use it to talk to their ancestors, and to people they've never met, and to people who haven't been born yet...
MARY:	Ghosts?
BOB:	More than ghosts. It's a way of listening to a secret music that helps you live your life...you can feed off it, it gives you

	sustenance...but this is the difficult bit for us to get hold of... Aboriginal people see
their	dreamtime as normal and natural. Whereas your average white man thinks it's crazy. Your Ralphy would think it's crazy.
MARY:	What about your average white woman?
BOB:	There's nothing average about you, white woman.
MARY:	Good God. A compliment. Do you want a receipt?
BOB:	Do you think I'm crazy? To believe in dreamtime?
MARY:	I've always thought you were a bit crazy. But I don't see why the Aboriginal people of Australia should take the blame.

(RALPH calls to them from the living room area.)

RALPH: Cocoa's ready.

BOB: (To MARY) Spoken like an average white man.

RALPH: Do you drink cocoa, Bob?

BOB: Hardly ever drink anything else, man, Ralphy.

MARY: *(To BOB)* He hates being called Ralphy.

BOB: Noted.

(MARY gets up from the bench and heads towards the living area.)

BOB: Be with you in a minute.

(MARY reacts, then crosses to RALPH. Fade lights on living room area. Focus on BOB. A little music.

Lights on FATHER, a distance from BOB,
still in his uniform.)

FATHER: Are you all right, son?
BOB: Not really.
FATHER: What's up with you, man?
BOB: You.
FATHER: I might have guessed it.
BOB: The last thing you said to me was...
FATHER: *(Breaks in)* Look after your mother.
BOB: Right.
FATHER: And so you did. For a while.
BOB: But I wasn't here when it mattered, was I?
FATHER: Mary was here.
BOB: And I was on the other side of the world.
Fighting battles for you, as a matter of fact.
FATHER: I never asked you to fight battles for me.
BOB: If you'd asked me to, likely I wouldn't have
bothered.

(A little music.)

FATHER: And what else are you dreaming about, son?
BOB: My secret.
FATHER: I won't tell.
BOB: A kid I played football with a million years
ago. And a little lass in a red hat who used
to come and watch.
FATHER: Ye bugger. Mustn't get between a man and
dreams of that kind.

(Lights out on FATHER.
Lights up on living room area as BOB
crosses to MARY and RALPH at the table.)

RALPH: Are you all right, Bob?
BOB: Certainly. Why should I not be all right?

27

*(BOB senses - correctly no doubt - that
MARY and RALPH have been talking about
him.)*

RALPH:	No reason just...I never realised the back yard was such a big attraction.
BOB:	Australia's an outdoor place. Big landscape. Big sky. Big country. You get out of the habit of rooms.
	(BOB takes a sip of his cocoa.)
BOB:	My, you make a canny drop of cocoa, Ralphy lad.
	(Corrects himself)
	Ralph.
RALPH:	I'm famous for it.
MARY:	And there's another big surprise for you.
BOB:	What? Bigger than the cocoa?
MARY:	*(To RALPH)* Tell him.
RALPH:	Tomorrow. Do you fancy a conducted tour?
BOB:	Of what? The back yard?
RALPH:	The new Tyneside. I've arranged to take the day off work.
BOB:	You've taken the day off?
RALPH:	I've still got a few days due.
BOB:	However will the Abbey National survive?
MARY:	Shut up, man, and listen.
BOB:	I'm listening.
RALPH:	There's nothing more to listen to. I've said it. Day off. Conducted tour. The new Tyneside.
BOB:	That's really grand. Thank you both.
	(Looks around the room.)
BOB:	Have you got a telephone directory?

*(MARY finds it, hands it to him.
BOB opens it. As BOB browses in
directory.)*

BOB:	Ye bugger. I didn't realise there were that many Turnbulls on Tyneside.
MARY:	They're right up there with the Robsons and Milburns.
RALPH:	You looking for somebody?
BOB:	He was sort of my best mate. We played for the same football team.
RALPH:	And he's called Turnbull?
BOB:	Yes. Kenny Turnbull. That's why I'm looking under Turnbull. There's always a bit of logic in what I do.
RALPH:	I can't help you. Unless he's changed his name to Marco Gabbiadini.
BOB:	Marco who?
RALPH:	Gabbiadini.
BOB:	Sounds like a raincoat.
RALPH:	Sunderland's striker.
BOB:	What they used to call a centre-forward when I was little?
RALPH:	What they used to call a centre-forward.
MARY:	If it's football, I'm going to bed.
BOB:	The really great ones used Brylcreem and had centre partings.
RALPH:	All footballers had centre partings.
BOB:	Apart from Jacky Milburn.
RALPH:	And the baldy-headed ones.
BOB:	Hey, there were some very good baldy-headed players...
RALPH:	We could pick a team.
BOB:	The world's greatest baldy-headed footballers, to play against Mars in the Inter-Galactic Cup. Sponsored by the Abbey National.

(MARY stands up and announces:)

MARY:	I am going to bed!

RALPH: Start off with the Charlton brothers.

                    (RALPH starts writing out his team sheet.)

BOB: Hughie Gallacher lost his hair, didn't he?
RALPH: By the time he played for Gateshead, yes,
                    I'm sure.

                    *(RALPH writes Hughie's name down.
                    BOB reacts to MARY.)*

BOB: I'm sorry, pet, you know how it is.
MARY: I've lived with it long enough.

                    (RALPH gets up.)

RALPH: Where's my Rothmans Football Annual?

                    (RALPH looks for his Rothmans.)

BOB: *(To RALPH)* I think you'll find Grimsby
                    Town had a bald-headed goalkeeper called
                    George Tweedy.

                    (RALPH finds the book. Starts browsing.)

RALPH: That's good. The goalkeeper could be a
                    problem.

                    (He's now totally absorbed in the game.)

BOB: *(To MARY)* See? Providing you stick to
                    football, Ralphy's got his dreamtime.
MARY: I already knew that.
BOB: I think that's about his limit, though.
MARY: I like him better that way.
RALPH: Ray Wilkins...Ralph Coates...Terry

Mancini...hang on, if it's a World Eleven, we can have Brazilians and Italians...I need my other books...

(He goes off in search of more books.)

MARY: I need sleep.

(She goes off in search of sleep. BOB addresses audience.)

BOB: I needed time and space and Kenny Turnbull's telephone number.

(A little music fades in, punctuating BOB'S soliloquy: gentle and plaintive, music that sings of searching - maybe ON GREEN DOLPHIN STREET?)

BOB: I decided Kenny Turnbull could wait until tomorrow. Or the day after.
(Throws telephone directory aside.)
Theoretically he could wait for ever. We hadn't spoken to each other for thirty years so forty-eight hours wouldn't make a Hell of a lot of difference. He might have moved to West Hartlepool. He might be dead. Or any point between, if you can find a point between West Hartlepool and death.

(Behind him, RALPH enters and prepares the 'car' - which need be no more than an arrangement of chairs.)

BOB: Ralph was up early next day. I'd got the feeling he was up early every day. He'd picked his baldy-headed team. He fastened the team sheet to the fridge door with a little magnetic frog. Not a bad side, either. A bit susceptible to high crosses from the left. I explained that to him. He said he'd look into it.

Then he started preparations for the great conducted tour of Tyneside. He washed the car. Can you believe that? Washed the car. When I was a lad the only person we knew that had a car was Uncle George. He'd gone through the card at Gosforth Park the day of the Northumberland Plate. He spent his winnings on an old Ford and he never washed it. He reckoned six layers of muck were the best protection against the pollution in the atmosphere. Course, it wasn't called pollution then. Pollution hadn't been invented. It was just muck. The only answer to muck is more muck, he used to say. He should have been a newspaper proprietor.

(MARY enters, crosses to RALPH at the car.)

MARY:	Are we ready yet?
RALPH:	Just about.

(BOB turns to join them.)

BOB:	Have you got the flask and the banana sandwiches?
RALPH:	There's plenty of places to eat.
BOB:	The pie and pea shop?
MARY:	You'll be lucky.
RALPH:	Anything you fancy. Italian, Indian,

	Chinese, French, Greek, Japanese...
BOB:	I can get all those in Sydney. What about Geordie?
MARY:	Beamish Museum's probably your best bet.

(RALPH does a final polish of the car.)

RALPH: I think we're ready.

BOB: *(To audience)* It was a sensible car. Volkswagen. Two years old. One previous owner. A very careful owner. Ralphy had checked on various computers. It used to belong to a mother superior. She only used it to drive to the altar and back six times a day. Plus one trip to Lourdes when her knees were playing up.

(By which time they're all three in the car. RALPH switches on the motor.)

RALPH: All right. Where do you want to go?
BOB: What?
RALPH: Where do you want to go?
BOB: It's your conducted tour, not mine.
RALPH: I mean, I can take you anywhere...
MARY: We thought you might have opinions. I mean, you've got opinions about everything else.
BOB: All right. Take me to Penshaw Hill.
MARY: Penshaw Hill. Off we go.
RALPH: I don't know where it is.
BOB: Jesus Christ.
             (Music: maybe a little paraphrase of THE LAMBTON WORM.
             Against this:)

BOB:	There was no problem. Ralphy had his map with him. Tell you the truth, I think he has his map with him when he goes to the netty.
	(Music continues. *They get out of the car and climb the* *hill. Again, we don't need the real thing or* *anything like it - just a bit of elevation, and* *a bit of wind on the air.* *Music fades in and out of the following:)*
BOB:	I came here with my Mam and Dad. On a picnic.
MARY:	With a flask of tea and banana sandwiches?
BOB:	Probably. Except it must have been during the war, and you couldn't get bananas during the war. So I must have made it up about the banana sandwiches.
RALPH.	How did you get here?
BOB:	Must have been on the bus. Unless it was Uncle George's car. But you couldn't get petrol in the war so...
MARY:	You must have made that up as well.
BOB:	But I remember my Dad bringing me here so he could teach me to count.
RALPH:	Count? You mean like...one, two, three?
	(Again at a distance, a light on MOTHER *and FATHER, the latter in uniform.)*
FATHER:	See how many pitheads you can count. One...
BOB:	One...
FATHER:	Two...
BOB:	Two...
FATHER:	Three...

BOB:	Three...
FATHER:	There's Boldon and Birtley and Silksworth...
BOB:	*(To MARY and RALPH)* He knew all the names of all the pit villages in the entire county...
MARY:	And they're still in your bones?
BOB:	You bet.
FATHER:	Shildon and Blackhall, Seaham and Easington.
BOB:	Wingate and Cramlington, Trimdon and Langley Park.
FATHER:	And they give pretty names to the collieries...St Hilda's, Dean and Chapter...
MOTHER:	Tell the lad why they do that.
FATHER:	Should I?
BOB:	Why do they give them pretty names, Dad?
FATHER:	Because men get killed in the pit.
BOB:	Men get killed in the army an' all, don't they, Dad?
MOTHER:	Hush.
FATHER:	Aye, they do.
BOB:	All gone?

(Lights out on MOTHER and FATHER. BOB is once more on the hill with MARY and RALPH.)

MARY:	What?
BOB:	The collieries? The pit villages? All gone?
MARY:	Mostly. There's maybe half a dozen pits left but not so's you'd notice.
BOB:	Don't tell me. Closed down in the cause of productivity and efficiency.
MARY:	Yes.

RALPH:	Strictly speaking, it's correct.
BOB:	Is it? Strictly speaking?
RALPH;	Well...yes.

(RALPH realises BOB is challenging him, but isn't sure if he wants to meet it.)

BOB:	So what do people do for work?
RALPH:	There's Nissan.
BOB:	The mighty yen.
RALPH:	It's the way it is.
BOB:	Shouldn't working people have the choice?
RALPH:	They do.
BOB:	Nissan or the dole?
MARY;	My Dad had the choice. He could be killed in the pit or killed in the army, He chose the army.

(Pause. Musical punctuation.)

| BOB: | Let's go and look at the river. |

(He goes to the car. RALPH and MARY follow. Music sets them on their way. Then, as they're driving along:)

BOB:	Have I told you about Japan's great Australian project?
RALPH:	Are Nissan going to build a car factory in Australia?
BOB:	Ralphy, man. *(Corrects himself)* Ralph, my friend. We're not talking about County Durham. We're talking about Australia. It's the size of Europe with a population of sixteen million, give or take the odd

	whingeing Pommy bastard. Got those statistics in your head?
RALPH:	Certainly.
BOB:	Right then. The project. The Japanese give every card-carrying Australian a million dollars. That's it. That's the project.

(RALPH and MARY are both baffled.)

MARY:	Doesn't sound much of a project to me. What do the Japanese get?
BOB:	Australia.
RALPH:	Australia?
BOB:	Yes.
MARY:	Then what happens?
BOB:	It's up to them. They've bought it. They can do what they like with it.
RALPH:	What sort of thing?
BOB:	Sink a few shafts. Dig out the gold. Fill up the holes with nuclear waste.
RALPH:	You're kidding.
BOB:	Build golf courses and theme parks with simulated volcanoes and tea houses. Battery farms to breed raw fish. Who cares? It belongs to them now.
MARY:	I suppose you've worked it all out.
BOB:	All you need's a pocket calculator, an atlas and a copy of the Wall Street Journal. Imperialism without gunboats. You know it makes sense.
MARY:	So when do you get your million dollars?
BOB:	That's the catch. The working people never get the million dollars.
RALPH:	Oh, you're just playing games, man.
BOB:	You think Nissan's a game? *(He yells to the world.)*

Hold up your hand if you've collected
your million dollars yet!

(To RALPH and MARY.)
See? They're all still waiting to collect.

*(Then BOB gets out of the car and walks
down front, addressing the audience.)*

BOB: Then we looked at the river.

*(RALPH and MARY join him. A little music
runs through this sequence.)*

BOB: The waters of Tyne.
RALPH: Cleaner than they used to be.
BOB: Fancy a swim?
RALPH: Forgot to bring a towel.
BOB: Is it all right if I try a few more names on
                  you?
MARY: No harm in trying.
BOB: Swan Hunter, Reyrolle, Hawthorn Leslie,
                  Armstrong, Clarke Chapman, Palmer...
MARY: Not quite all gone. Still one or two left.
BOB: Palmer's shipyard of Jarrow-on-Tyne.
RALPH: Well, obviously, Palmer's went years ago.
BOB: Something just came into my mind.
MARY: I daresay there's plenty room for it.
BOB: A few years ago, I was working on a
                  building site in North Queensland. It's a bit
                  like the Wild West. Except it's North.
MARY: Being Australia, you'd expect to find the
                  West in the North, I suppose.
RALPH: No. I think what Bob told us was you find
                  the North in the South and the East in the
                  West.
MARY: What happened in North Queensland?
                  Wherever it is.

BOB:	I met a young trade unionist. Early twenties. Never been out of Australia. Only just out of nappies. He knew three things about England. He knew about the Royal Family, though he wasn't sure about any of their names. I couldn't help him much. He knew about the bodyline bowling cricket tour, meaning he knew Harold Larwood was a great bowler and Douglas Jardine was an arrogant upper-class bastard. And he knew about Palmer's of Jarrow. The whole story.
MARY:	The town that was murdered.
BOB:	Knew the story. Every last detail. Every last bolt and rivet.
MARY:	How did he know?
BOB:	In his bones.
MARY:	Dreamtime?
BOB:	I daresay.

(Pause. Maybe an odd siren from the river. A little musical coda as they cross to the car. They drive on. As they do so:)

BOB:	Question. Who builds the ships now?
MARY:	The mighty yen?
BOB:	Next question. Who owns the ships now?
MARY:	The mighty yen?
BOB:	Question. If Jarrow in the 1920's was a company town, are we now in the 1990's turning into a company world?
MARY:	You want me to say yes, don't you? I can tell.
BOB:	I'd very much like you to say yes.
MARY:	The world that was murdered?
BOB:	No. This time it'll be suicide.
RALPH:	It'll have to be ritual suicide, won't it? Isn't that part of the corporate image?

BOB:	Stop making racist jokes. Concentrate on your driving.
RALPH:	I would if I knew where I was going.
BOB:	I need a drink. Find us the pub.
RALPH:	How do you mean? The pub?
BOB:	The one that's left. Is there one left?

(They get out of the car and cross to a pub table.)

BOB:	*(To audience)* We went to the Crown Posada. It was still there, in the same place. I got the drinks in. *(Quick exit then returns instantly with a tray of drinks. To audience)* What's more, I think the service is quicker than it used to be. *(Takes drinks to the table.)* Vodka and tonic for you, pet...(MARY)...half a pint of alcohol-free lager for you...(RALPH)
RALPH:	Only because I'm driving.
BOB:	Don't worry, man. I'm not casting aspersions on your virility. I could tell, first minute I saw you, this is a hard-drinking man. And I'll try to struggle through this pint.

(He sits down at the table with his pint.)

	Cheers.
RALPH:	Cheers.
MARY:	Cheers.
BOB:	And thank you.
RALPH:	You bought the drinks.
BOB:	For the conducted tour.
RALPH:	I'm only sorry you found it depressing.
MARY:	Things change.
BOB:	Can we do the check list now?

MARY:	Do whatever you like. You're the visitor. Also my brother. We're supposed to be polite to you.
BOB:	All right... so the pits have gone and most of the ship-building's gone...but I can throw stones at global capitalism and that makes me feel a bit better. It's a big fight but there's always a return clause in the contract.
RALPH:	What check list?
BOB:	Hi there Ralph, nice to have you with us.
RALPH:	No, I was thinking about something else.
MARY:	What were you thinking about?
RALPH:	Don Howe and Pop Robson.
MARY:	Who are they?
RALPH:	A bald-headed full-back and a bald-headed striker.
BOB:	Excellent. We'll have them in the squad. Get their names down.

(BOB hands him a beermat. RALPH notes the names.)

RALPH:	Great.
MARY:	Check list.
BOB:	Right. I want to know which bits of canny Newcastle are still left. On account of from what I've seen most of it's gone.
MARY:	Like what?
BOB:	Like The Royal Oak.
MARY:	Gone.
BOB:	The Dun Cow.
MARY:	Gone. To make way for university expansion.
RALPH:	And you must be in favour of that.
BOB:	Depends on the syllabus.
MARY:	Get on with your list, man.

BOB:	I could go for ever with pubs. Let's move on. Culture.
MARY:	You? Culture?
BOB:	The Palace Theatre, where I saw Max Wall.
MARY:	Demolished for redevelopment.
BOB:	The Grand at Byker, where I saw Bobby Thompson.
MARY:	Ditto.
BOB:	The Empire, where I saw Jimmy James, the greatest comedian in the history of the human race.
RALPH:	Jimmy who?
BOB:	Baldy-headed comedian. Put him on the team. He'll be good value.
MARY:	Demolished to make way for offices and a hotel.
BOB:	This'll impress you. The Jesmond Playhouse, where I once went to see a play by George Bernard Shaw because the comrades said he was handy with the jokes as well as being ideologically sound.
MARY:	Demolished to make way for road improvements that never happened.
BOB:	Par for the course. What about Eldon Square?
MARY:	Half gone.
BOB:	The Royal Arcade?
MARY:	They knocked it down and kept the bits. They were going to re-erect it but the stones got left out in the rain. It washed off the chalk marks.
RALPH:	Chalk marks?
MARY:	The chalk marks were there to explain how to put it back together again.
BOB:	Moving into middle-class gentility... what happened to Brandling Park?
MARY:	Buried under a motorway.
BOB:	The Old Assembly Rooms, where I danced

	the night away to Willie Walker's Band?
MARY:	Casino.
BOB:	The Oxford Galleries where I danced the night away to the George Evans Orchestra?
MARY:	Disco.
BOB:	The billiard halls? There used to be one in Northumberland Street. It had scenes from Greek and Roman mythology on the walls. It's where I got my classical education.
MARY:	I'm no expert but I think they've all gone.
RALPH:	I believe there's some rather nice snooker centres.

(BOB makes a face.)

BOB:	Snooker centres?
RALPH:	With decor and such.
BOB:	Carpets and rubber plants?
RALPH:	Yes.
BOB:	Can you imagine that? Billiard halls with interior designers?

(He finishes his beer and gets up.)

| BOB: | Same again? |

(Doesn't wait for an answer but exits and again returns instantly with a loaded tray.)

| BOB: | That lass behind the bar, she's amazing. She's got the order all ready waiting every time I go to the bar, and the right change from a five pound note including half of shandy for herself. |

(He distributes the drinks as before. Then sits down.)

BOB:	Tell you something else. The last time I was in here, you could get a round of drinks without using paper money at all. Happy days. Cheers.
MARY:	Cheers.
RALPH:	Cheers.

BOB:	And I'm sorry. I apologise.
MARY:	You apologise?
BOB:	Sincerely.
RALPH:	What for?
MARY:	*(To RALPH)* I can't smell anything, can you?
BOB:	For being such a miserable bugger. You give me the conducted tour and all I do is moan.
MARY:	Maybe there's something to moan about. Maybe one of us agrees with you.
BOB:	But it's bad manners, isn't it? What would our Mam say?
MARY:	She'd say it was bad manners.
RALPH:	Drink up!

(RALPH stands up, very decisive.)

BOB:	What?
RALPH:	We're moving on.
BOB:	Is your husband usually this decisive?
MARY:	Only when I tell him.
RALPH:	There's something I want you to see.
BOB:	O.K. Lead the way, action man.

*(They drink up and leave the table.
BOB addresses the audience.)*

BOB: We got in Ralphy's safe little motor car and he drove us across the river to Gateshead. Except what we saw didn't look like Gateshead at all.

*(He joins MARY and RALPH as they walk
through the Metro Centre.
A combination of pretty lights, overlapping
muzaks and corporate imagery.
They look around them with a range of
reactions: RALPH is impressed, MARY*

phlegmatic, BOB working it all out, as
usual.)

BOB: What's this? A Palace of Culture?
MARY: The Hall of the Mountain King.
BOB: Never-never land.
MARY: Spot on.
BOB: Does it have a name?
RALPH: It's called the Metro Centre.
BOB: I remember when it was called Gateshead.
RALPH: It's the biggest commercial complex in the
            whole of Europe.

            (Long pause.
            Music and lighting effects build.
            Then a sudden silence and:)

BOB: Well it's basically a big shop, isn't it?
MARY: Like I said. Never-never land.
BOB: *(To MARY)* Take me home, pet.

            (Cross-fade to living-room.
            RALPH is clearing the table.
            MARY is reading the paper.
            BOB has the telephone directory open on
            his knee as he dials a number.
            He waits for a reply then:)

BOB: *(On phone)*
            Hello, you don't know me, well you might
            know me, I'm not sure...I'm here on a visit
            from Australia and I'm trying to get in
            touch with my old mate Kenny Turnbull
            and I'm like working through the
            telephone book and I saw your number
            and...
            (Breaks off, listens, reacts then:)
            I see. I'm sorry I bothered you.

(He hangs up.)

MARY:	Wrong one?
BOB:	The woman that answered was married to Mr Kenneth Turnbull.
MARY:	*Your* Kenneth Turnbull?
BOB:	Apparently he died last month. So I didn't like to ask. I mean, you can't say: please accept my condolences and did he used to play right full-back for a football team in Walkergate?
MARY:	Try the next one.
BOB:	I'm wasting my time. That sort of thing puts you off. I always hated the telephone.
RALPH:	People who weren't brought up with telephones find them intimidating. I read that somewhere.
BOB:	You would.
MARY:	Go on, man, try again.
BOB:	Just to please you.
	(BOB dials the next number.
	He waits for the reply then:)
BOB:	Hell's teeth, it's an answering machine...
	(Recites what he's hearing)
	Mr Turnbull is unable to come to the phone right now, but if you'd like to leave your name and number he'll get back to you as soon as possible. Please speak after the bleep. Bleep.
	Hello, my name's Bob Rutherford, I'm over from Australia and I'm looking for Kenny Turnbull. We served our time together and we played full-back for Walkergate Dynamos. We also heard Louis Armstrong at the City Hall, watched United from the Gallowgate and went to the Oxford Galleries. Or the Old Assembly Rooms if we had our best suits on.

MARY:	Never mind the life story, just leave your name and number.
BOB:	Oh yes, sorry. I'm staying in Heaton and the number is... *(Checks)*...265-4696... *(Hangs up.)*
BOB:	I hate those things.
RALPH:	I think it was Readers Digest.
BOB:	What was?
RALPH:	Where I read it. About people being intimidated by the telephone.
BOB:	Thank you. I'd been worrying about that.
RALPH:	It's a good magazine. Always full of interesting little facts.
BOB:	Why don't you concentrate on baldy-headed footballers? I'm still a bit unhappy about the left side of midfield.
RALPH:	Leave it with me, Bob.

(RALPH gets on with his football research. BOB looks at telephone directory.)

BOB:	One last try. That'll make twenty. Enough phone calls for one night. Enough for a lifetime.
MARY:	And then we'll have cocoa.
RALPH:	*(Buried in Rothmans)* Soon as I've checked this. I think I'm on to something.

(BOB dials a number. He waits for the reply then:)

BOB:	Hello, you don't know me, I'm on a visit from Australia, I left Tyneside thirty years ago and I'm trying to get in touch with my old mate Kenny Turnbull.. *(Reacts)* ...No, I'm not trying to sell you double-glazing.. *(Reacts)* And I'm not trying to sell you cavity wall

insulation either, I'm not
trying to sell you anything, I'm only...
(Breaks off again and listens, then:)
...and I'm definitely not asking you to talk
dirty, why should I ask you to talk
dirty?.. *(Listens, reacts then:)*
...I am *not* a nuisance phone caller, I am *not*
a pervert, I am *not* a flasher...
(He hangs up.)

MARY: That seemed to go well.
BOB: She's going to report me to the police. Get
           them to trace the call.
           *(BOB throws the telephone directory away
           and gets up.)*
           I mean to say, what the Hell is going on?
           Everybody's either gone out, or gone crazy,
           or gone...dead.
MARY: Be fair. Some of them are watching
           pornographic videos.
RALPH: Jim Iley.
BOB: No, I'm looking for Kenny Turnbull.
RALPH: He could be the left-sided midfield player
           we're looking for. Extremely bald. I'm going
           back a few years, like. I think they were
           still called wing-halves when Jim Iley was
           playing.
BOB: Correction. Either out, or crazy, or dead, or
           watching porno movies...or playing silly
           bloody games.
MARY: I'm reading the Evening Chronicle.
BOB: You're all right, pet. It's the others. I'll be
           in the back yard.

           (BOB goes out into the back yard.
           He sits down on the bench.
           Reactions from MARY and RALPH.)

RALPH: Is it something I said?

MARY: It's not your fault pet.

RALPH: I don't want to upset you but, is it maybe
            him that's crazy?

MARY: It's a point of view.

RALPH: I wondered. I mean, he's canny. I really like
            him.

MARY: Ralph. You are an amazing man.

RALPH: Am I?

            (MARY nods.)

RALPH: Thank you.

            *(Cross-fade to BOB, on the bench.
            He's isolated in a pool of light.)*

BOB: I'm sorry, Dad. I shouldn't have gone away.
            You turn your back for five minutes...all
            right, thirty years...and it all goes wrong.
            You remember our bonny Tyneside? Well it
            isn't bonny any more. Somebody poisoned
            the water in the river but I don't know his
            name.
            (He looks across into the darkness.)
            Dad? I don't know what to do. I am fifty
            years old, and I am frightened, and I don't
            know what to do. Dad?

            *(A light in the darkness, but he doesn't see
            his father.
            Instead, he sees SHEILA: a girl in her late
            teens, leaning on a bicycle. She wear a
            raincoat and a red beret perched on the side
            of her head - a little bit saucy like...)*

BOB: Sheila!

49

(She raises her hand in a discreet wave.
BOB waves back.
Against this a few bars of BODY AND SOUL.
RALPH comes into the yard.)

RALPH: Bob.
BOB: *(Half-turn)* Be with you in a minute.
RALPH: Phone call for you.
BOB: Just a minute I said!

(He turns again to look at SHEILA but she's
gone. All that's left is darkness.
BOB'S attention switches to RALPH.)

BOB: A phone call?
RALPH: Kenny Turnbull for you.
BOB: Ye bugger.

(Cross-fade to living room as BOB goes into
the house.
MARY hands him the phone.)

BOB: Hello.

(KENNY in a pool of light across the stage.
He's expensively half-dressed - trousers and
unbuttoned shirt. He's speaking on a
portable telephone.)

KENNY: Is that little Bobby?
BOB: I suppose it must be.
KENNY: Back from the colonies? Is that right?
BOB: That's right.
KENNY: Made your fortune?
BOB: No.
KENNY: Little Bobby Rutherford. Man, I can't believe
it. I was just getting down to a bit of
business here when my bleeper went off...

BOB:	Business? Bleeper?
KENNY:	You know? Business? Negotiating a merger, like? *(Turns to somebody off-stage.)* I'll be right with you, pet. *(Then to BOB.)*
KENNY:	I've got this bleeper, see. It goes off when anybody leaves a message on the answering machine. It's great, man.
BOB:	I daresay.
KENNY:	So when am I going to see you?
BOB:	How about the match tomorrow? Do you still go?
KENNY:	Do I still go? For God's sake, man, Bobby, we hold certain truths to be self-evident. *(Again reacts to off-stage girl.)* Hinny, if you're getting impatient, start without me and I'll catch up.
BOB:	Great. So I'll meet you in The Strawberry? Two o'clock?
KENNY:	You've got to be joking, Bob.
BOB:	They haven't knocked it down, have they?
KENNY:	Listen. This is a big reunion. We'll do it in style.
BOB:	Style?
KENNY:	You get all sorts in The Strawberry. No, I'll pick you up in one of my nice shiny motor cars. *(Looks off-stage.)* Eee pet, you didn't learn that in Hexham. *(Lights out on KENNY.* *BOB steps forward to audience.)*
BOB:	Kenny picked me up in a nice shiny motor car. The native population of Heaton had never seen such a vehicle. It stuck out at

both ends of the street. It was big enough to
sub-let.

*(BOB puts on a very old black and white
scarf. A bit of Going-To-The-Match music.
Cross-fade as BOB joins KENNY walking the
last few yards to the ground.
KENNY has his jacket and tie on now. No
scarf.)*

KENNY: Nice set of wheels, eh?
BOB: Very impressive. Big car though. Do you not
            have trouble parking?
KENNY: When you drive a car like mine, you park
            where you bloody well like.

(Crowd noise.)

BOB: Do you remember the last game we saw?
            Before I went to Oz?
KENNY: No.
BOB: We won seven-two.
KENNY: It must have been a long time ago.
BOB: Against Fulham.
KENNY: Fulham? That proves it was a long time ago.
            I think they play in the Church League now.
BOB: Man, I'd forgotten the sound a football
            match makes ten minutes before the kick-
            off.

(As the crowd noise builds.)

KENNY: Don't worry.
BOB: I'm not worried.
KENNY: Here we are.

*(He leads BOB into an executive box - either
flown or trucked in.*

The crowd noise cuts off completely. BOB is totally baffled.)

BOB: What the Hell's this?
KENNY: It's my executive box.
BOB: Your what?
KENNY: My executive box.
BOB: Does this go with the shiny motor car?
KENNY: Aye, it's all part of the set, bonny lad. Not to mention this...

(He produces a bottle of champage from an ice bucket, plus two glasses.
BOB watches, bewildered, as KENNY opens the bottle and pours two glasses of champagne.)

BOB: But we're at a football match.
KENNY: Certainly we're at a football match.
BOB: What's wrong with the Gallowgate?
KENNY: Look at it. You want to stand with the animals, that's up to you. Me, if I want to see animals, I go to a safari park. Here. Sup up.
           (He hands BOB some champagne.
           BOB takes it, sips it warily.)
KENNY: Up yours.
BOB: Cheers.
KENNY: Sit down. Make yourself at home.

(BOB sits down, but he isn't at home.)

BOB: So what do you have to do to get an executive box?
KENNY: Same as you do to get anything. You give the man some money.
BOB: Does that mean you're an executive?
KENNY: My card.

(KENNY hands BOB a card. BOB reads it.)

BOB: Bede Investments PLC. Chairman....Kenneth Turnbull. What's PLC?

KENNY: It's what used to be And Company Limited. PLC stands for... *(Ponders)*...what the Hell *does* it stand for? Public Liability Company. But as far as I'm concerned, it stands for Piles of Lovely Cash.

BOB: I see. And what do they do?

KENNY: What do who do?

BOB: Bede Investments PLC?

KENNY: Real Estate. Demolition. Building.

BOB: So you're the one?

KENNY: I'm the one what? Stop talking in riddles, man.

BOB: You're the one knocking down Tyneside and replacing it with plastic imitations?

KENNY: I'm not the only one. But I'm one of the ones. I knock down as much as I can lay my hands on.

BOB: I see. I think.

KENNY: Here. Have some more champagne. Don't suppose you get much of this in Australia.

BOB: It may come as a surprise, but in Australia working men can afford to drink champagne and eat oysters.

KENNY: Well, it doesn't apply in England. We've nearly abolished working men. It's the executive box or the animal enclosure. There's not much in between.

(BOB sits back, trying to absorb all this. Then stands up as the teams come out.)

BOB: Howay the lads! Howay United!

(KENNY remains seated and silent.)

KENNY:	What are you doing?
BOB:	Newcastle United have taken the field. I've travelled thirteen thousand miles for this.
KENNY:	No point in shouting. They can't hear you.
BOB:	That's not the point.
KENNY:	Animals shout. Executives sit back, sipping their champagne, like gentlemen. Every so often, we might avert the gaze ever so slightly towards the pitch and murmur...oh I say, well played sir.
BOB:	You're kidding.
KENNY:	Less than you might think.
BOB:	But if you're busy boozing, you might miss something.
KENNY:	If we miss something, we watch the replay on our personal television monitor.

(He directs BOB'S attention to the television monitor. BOB sits down, takes a sip of champagne, and tries to watch the match KENNY'S way.)

BOB:	What's that written on their shirts?
KENNY:	Sponsor's name.
BOB:	Don't know why I bothered asking.
KENNY:	These days, anything that moves can get a sponsor. Get a sponsor or die.
BOB:	The Natwest winger takes a corner, the Hanson Trust striker beats the British Telecom goalkeeper with a header but the ball's cleared off the line by the Benson and Hedges fullback.
KENNY:	See? You do understand. *(He leans forward.)* Oh, I say, well played there, Quinn.
BOB:	That isn't Quinn.
KENNY:	So?

(They watch in silence for while, BOB wanting to shout but not doing so, KENNY drinking.)

BOB: We served our time together on the building site.

KENNY: Happy days.

BOB: We joined the union on the same day.

KENNY: That's right, brother.

BOB: And the Young Socialists.

KENNY: The people's flag is deepest red, comrade.

BOB: And we called our team the Walkergate Dynamos after the Moscow Dynamos.

KENNY: As a gesture of solidarity with the great Soviet Socialist revolution.

BOB: If you weren't in the party, you couldn't play for the team.

KENNY: I know.

BOB: So what happened?

KENNY: Well, among other things, we finished bottom of the league.

BOB: No. What happened to *you*?

KENNY: That's easy. I looked around the building site one day and I thought, I am on the wrong end of the bit of string. Somebody is operating me, like a puppet. I climbed up the bit of string. I am the master now.

BOB: Traded your cloth cap for a bowler hat?

KENNY: No, Bobby, not a bowler. Toppers or nothing.

BOB: You? In a top hat?

KENNY: When the kids got married, certainly. Topper and tails. What do you expect? Ham salad from the Co-op ?

(BOB gets up and crosses to the door of the box.)

KENNY: Where you going?
BOB: The Gallowgate. I don't belong here.
KENNY: I'm not sure you belong there.
BOB: We'll see.

            (BOB leaves the box.
            He hears the noise of the crowd: the jungle
            style chanting directed at an opposing black
            player. BOB goes back into the box, closing
            the noise out.)

BOB: What's that noise I heard?
KENNY: The lads doing their jungle noises?
BOB: Something of the sort.
KENNY: Hang on.
            (Leans forward, checks the pitch.)
            Their number seven. He's a coon.
BOB: He's what?
KENNY: You know. A coon. A coloured cousin. A
            black bastard. You've got them in Australia,
            haven't you? Or did you kill them off?

            (BOB stares at him. Then he walks out of
            the scene, downstage, and addresses the
            audience.
            KENNY sits there, sipping champagne,
            leaning forward from time to time, like an
            English gentleman in the pavilion at Lords.)

BOB: I did a thing I'd never done the whole of
            my life. I left a football match before the
            final whistle. And I'll tell you some other
            things I didn't do. I didn't go on to the
            Gallowgate and tell those lads to stop it. I
            might have taken them on one at a time but
            I've got a sentimental attachment to my
            head.
            And I didn't explain to Kenny about the

Aboriginal people and dreamtime. I didn't
ask him if he'd found true happiness in the
destruction of canny Newcastle. I didn't ask
him about his wife and kids. I didn't even
hit him and that's what I wanted to do. I
didn't do any of those things.
Instead, I behaved like a true native-born
Geordie with an Australian passport. I said
to the band...
(Turns to the band.)
...play me some good, dirty, low-down, go-
to-Hell blues. And I went off to dream about
a girl in a red hat...and find myself
something decent to drink.

*(He hurls the champagne glass at the
executive box. The band plays the blues.
BOB exits.)*

END OF ACT ONE

ACT TWO

*Band plays a little end-of-interval medley
with a bias towards ballads.*

*Maybe they end with I'M OLD-FASHIONED.
Lights on BOB, MARY and RALPH, sitting
on the bench in the back yard.*

*BOB and MARY are staring into space.
RALPH is reading the Saturday night
Pink 'Un.*

MARY: Well, now I've heard everything.
BOB: How do you mean?
MARY: You. Leaving a football match before the
           final whistle.
BOB: I didn't even stay till halftime.
MARY: Unbelievable.
BOB: I mean, when you discover your best mate's
           turned into a capitalist hyena. I remember
           the time Kenny wanted to hang people like
           that. And now he's turned into one. He'd
           even chosen his lamp-posts.
MARY: Lamp-posts?
BOB: When we were in the Young Socialists.
           We'd walk home from the pub and he'd
           pick out all the best lamp-posts. That's

	where we'll hang the capitalist hyenas, he'd
	say. When the revolution comes. And
	now he's got his own executive box.
MARY:	His revolution must have come.
BOB:	It certainly has. With knobs on. And then
	he says: you don't want to be out there on
	the terraces with the animals...and I go out
	there...and they're acting like animals. He's
	right. The whole world's gone to Hell.
RALPH:	Darlington did well today, mind.

(BOB reacts to this.)

BOB:	Well that's all right then, isn't it?
RALPH:	Good result.
BOB:	The glorious revolution lies in ruins. The
	dreams of a generation have turned into a
	nightmare. The working class sinking in the
	slime of its own betrayal. But never mind,
	lads, Darlington got a result.
RALPH:	And they were a goal down after twenty
	minutes.
BOB:	Mary. Your husband is an amazing man.
MARY:	Yes. I know. And you are a miserable sod.
BOB:	True.

(RALPH returns to his close scrutiny of his paper.)

MARY:	You didn't used to be.
BOB:	What? Miserable?
MARY:	You used to be fairly cheerful. Except when
	you were trying to change the world.
BOB:	That always makes people miserable. Trying
	to change the world. When you think about
	them. Like, Jesus Christ and Karl Marx. Not
	famous for their jokes, either of them.
MARY:	Hitler?

BOB:	Not very funny at all. Neither was Mussolini.
MARY:	Napoleon.
BOB:	Stalin.
MARY:	Gandhi.
BOB:	Julius Caesar.
MARY:	Attila the Hun.
BOB:	Alexander the Great.
RALPH:	Keith Kettleborough.

(They react.)

MARY:	Who?
RALPH:	Keith Kettleborough.
MARY:	Don't tell me. A lesser-known revolutionary figure. Was he from Darlington?
RALPH:	No. He played for Newcastle United. Baldy-headed inside-forward. Roughly contemporary with Jim Iley. In fact, they looked similar at a casual glance, like. But on closer examination, Keith Kettleborough had rather more prominent teeth.
MARY:	I see.
BOB:	But not one of the world's great radical thinkers?
RALPH:	That I wouldn't know. But I think we should consider him for a place in our squad.
BOB:	In that case, I think so too. I'm very glad you mentioned it, Ralph.
RALPH:	My pleasure.

(RALPH goes back to his paper.
BOB and MARY trade reactions.)

BOB:	How long does it generally take him to read the paper on a Saturday night?

MARY:	From now until... *(checks her watch)...*
	until he gets his new one next Saturday.
BOB:	'Cause I was thinking, when he finishes, if
	he ever finishes, we could go out.

MARY:	Fine. Where do you want to go?
BOB:	Find a pub. Have a couple of pints.
MARY:	Game of darts?
BOB:	Does he play darts?
MARY:	No, but I do.
BOB:	Fish and chips on the way home?
MARY:	You're on.
	(The telephone rings in the house.)
MARY:	As soon as I've answered the phone.
BOB:	I don't even like the way telephones ring
	these days.

(As MARY goes into the house to answer the phone.)

BOB:	Like a canary with its leg trapped.
RALPH:	Norwich City.
BOB:	What?
RALPH:	Norwich City.
BOB:	I was talking about the telephone.
RALPH:	Canaries, you said. Norwich City are known
	as the Canaries.
BOB:	Thank you for the information.

(MARY returns.)

| MARY: | *(To BOB)* It's for you. |

(BOB gets up.)

BOB:	Excuse me, Ralph. I'm wanted on the
	telephone. It's a long distance from
	Norwich.

RALPH:	Two hundred and fifty-five miles.
BOB:	What?
RALPH:	But some of it's motorway.
BOB:	*(To MARY)* We've had him looked at but he hasn't been seen to.
	(BOB goes into the house.)
MARY:	What's all that about?
RALPH:	Canaries mostly.

(Cross-fade. BOB on the telephone in the house.
KENNY on his mobile phone somewhere in Tyne and Wear.)

KENNY:	Hey, man, what happened to you this afternoon?
BOB;	I left in disgust. Didn't you notice?
KENNY:	Tell you what. You missed a really terrible match.
BOB:	Good.
KENNY:	What do you mean? Good?
BOB:	Some things haven't changed.
KENNY:	So when are we going to see you again?
BOB:	Well, no offence but I thought, most likely, never.
KENNY:	Never? What are you talking about?
BOB:	I don't want to sound like Neighbours, man, but...well, things can never be the same again between you and me.
KENNY:	Bollocks.
BOB:	You and your big motor car and your executive box...
KENNY:	Listen...just 'cause you're an honest son of toil and I'm a ruthless, self-seeking, evil, capitalist, bastard shitehawk...we can still be friends. What you doing tonight?
BOB:	Going out.

KENNY:	Where you going? Who with?
BOB:	Going out with our Mary and Ralph. Couple of pints. Game of darts. Fish and chips.
KENNY:	We can do better than that.
BOB:	I don't want to do better than that. It's a proper night out for an honest Geordie son of toil.
KENNY:	I'll take you out to dinner.
BOB:	I've had my dinner.
KENNY:	Don't play the noble peasant with me, bonny lad. We're talking serious food and serious wine. None of your half-carafe of the house white if it isn't too dry.
BOB:	Maybe I'd rather have a couple of pints.
KENNY:	I want you to share the fruits of my labours.
BOB:	Not your labours. Other people's labours.
KENNY:	All right. I want to redistribute some of my wealth.
BOB:	But I'm going out with Mary and Ralph.
KENNY:	Bring them with you. Haven't seen your Mary for years. I don't know Ralph. Is he all right?

(BOB smiles.)

| BOB: | Oh aye. You'll enjoy Ralph. Laugh a minute. |

| KENNY: | Right then? |

(BOB hesitates briefly then:)

| BOB: | Right then. |

*(Music for a night on the town.
Anything from THE JOINT IS JUMPIN' to
Monk's LITTLE ROOTIE TOOTIE.*

BOB addresses audience as he puts on tie and jacket.)

BOB: I hate going out to places where you have to get changed before you can go out to them. I like going out to places where you can go as you are. But if Kenny wanted to share his profits with us, why should I try to stop him? I believe in profit-sharing. And if you're going to get legless, why not find a shitehawk to pick up the tab?

(Lights on a table set, elegantly and pretentiously, for five.)

BOB: It was a canny spot. Captain Pinkerton's Tandoori Pizzeria and Sushi House.

(RALPH and MARY, dressed in their best, join BOB as they are greeted by a WAITER in tuxedo.)

BOB: With a French waiter.
WAITER: Bon jour madame et messieurs.
BOB: *(To audience)* Sort of French.
(To WAITER) What part of Tynemouth do you come from, pet?
WAITER: The Latin Quarter.
RALPH: Is there a Latin Quarter in Tynemouth?
WAITER: Monsieur Turnbull's table.

(He sees them to the table and gives them very large menus to study. They sit down, already wondering whether it's a good idea.)

RALPH: Classy spot, isn't it?
MARY: Only the highest quality plastic.

(BOB leafs through the menu.)

BOB:	They certainly cater for all tastes. Japanese, Chinese, Italian, Jewish, French. All with rice or chips.
RALPH:	It says here...ethnic specialities. Pease pudding.
BOB:	What page is that?
MARY:	Chapter three. Verse fifteen.

(WAITER returns with champagne in a bucket.)

WAITER:	Champagne, madame, messieurs.
BOB:	We didn't order champagne, did we? Ralph. Did you order champagne?
RALPH:	I didn't order anything.
WAITER:	Avec les compliments of le management.
MARY:	On the house?
BOB:	Sur la maison.
WAITER:	*(To BOB)* Smartarse.
BOB:	It takes one to know one, monsieur.

(WAITER exits.)

BOB:	Let's get cracking, shall we?

(He pours champagne.)

RALPH:	They accept all major credit cards.
MARY:	Everything except money.
BOB:	You'll get away with yen. Did you bring your yen with you, Ralph?
RALPH:	I don't think I've ever seen a yen. Do they have a hole in the middle?
BOB:	You're thinking of bagels.

(A little Blue Note style fanfare from the

band as KENNY arrives.)

KENNY: *(To band)* Thanks lads.
          (He crosses to the table.)
          All settled in then?

BOB: Très bien, merci, monsieur.

KENNY: Can't beat all that foreign bollocks, can
          you? I mean, we're all Europeans now,
          aren't we? Mary. Good to see you again.
MARY: Is it?
KENNY: You haven't changed a bit. And this must be
          the legendary Ralph.
RALPH: What?

          *(KENNY sits down at the table and pours
          himself some champagne.)*

KENNY: Our lass is hanging her coat up. She'll be
          along in an hour or so. Are they looking
          after you all right?
BOB: Yes thank you.
KENNY: If they're not, just say the word and I'll
          sack somebody.
MARY: You own the place?
KENNY: Certainly I do.
BOB: I thought you were into demolition and
          redevelopment?
KENNY: I'm also into diversification. I've got a lot
          of eggs in a lot of baskets.
BOB: Well there's no need to sack anybody on
          our account. He's a very canny feller, that
          waiter.
KENNY: Jean Pierre?
MARY: Is that what he calls himself?
KENNY: And he's got a University degree.
RALPH: In French?

KENNY:	No. Philosophy.
BOB:	I'm told they make the best waiters.
KENNY:	He found out there wasn't much call for philosophers in Tynemouth. Certainly not for full-time professionals.
RALPH:	What about amateurs?
MARY:	Everybody's an amateur philosopher in Tynemouth. It fills the long winter evenings.
RALPH:	I'm not talking about philosophers.

(Before anybody finds out what RALPH is talking about, KENNY clicks his fingers at the band.)

KENNY: Howay lads. Get your fingers out.
(He turns to his guests at the table.)
We have live music on Fridays, Saturdays and Bank Holidays.
(Then turns to the band.)
Play pretty for the people. And for the woman born to be Queen.

(Band plays pretty music - say SOPHISTICATED LADY or MOOD INDIGO. SHEILA enters and crosses to the table. She's dressed well and expensively. She's not happy about the music and the fuss.)

SHEILA:	I asked you not to do that again.
KENNY:	Do you want me to sack the band?
SHEILA:	No. I want you to sack the chairman of the board.
KENNY:	Oh come on, lass. Here's Bobby come all the way from Australia. You're not going to spoil the evening for him and his family, are you?

(He turns to the others.)

I mean I think it's nice, don't you? Getting the band to play suitable music when regular customers come in? It's user-friendly. Now sit yourself down, pet, and say hello nicely to Bob and Mary and Ralph. My wife, Sheila.
(SHEILA hesitates, then sits down.)

SHEILA: Hello nicely, Bob, Mary, Ralph.
MARY: Hello Sheila.
RALPH: Hello Sheila.
BOB: G'day, Sheila.
SHEILA: Is that Australian?
BOB: Well done.
SHEILA: Just a lucky guess.

(KENNY tops up the glasses.)

KENNY: Right. Time for a toast. Any suggestions?
MARY: The Queen?

(With a look at SHEILA.)

RALPH: Tyneside?
BOB: Old Tyneside or New Tyneside?
KENNY: We could spend all night arguing about that.
MARY: I'm sure you will.
BOB: I remember the time when me and Kenny used to drink to Clause Four.
MARY: What's that? The sanity clause?
SHEILA: There ain't no sanity clause.
BOB: Clause Four of the Labour Party constitution. The workers will take over the means of production.
KENNY: Too late, Bobby. There are no means of production. There are no workers.
SHEILA: I think you should drink to your football team.

MARY:	Newcastle United?
SHEILA:	No.
RALPH:	Sunderland?
SHEILA:	Hardly.
BOB:	Darlington?
SHEILA:	No. Walkergate Dynamos.
MARY:	That's the team you two played for?

(Looking at BOB and KENNY.)

KENNY:	That's right. The meanest pair of full-backs that ever drew breath.
BOB:	Non pasaran.
KENNY:	They shall not pass.
BOB:	And they never did.
KENNY:	The ball did, like.
BOB:	But no winger ever lived to tell the tale.
KENNY:	We lost plenty of matches, like. But we never lost the body count.

(BOB looks hard at SHEILA.)

BOB:	And you're the lass in the little red hat that used to come and watch.
SHEILA:	On my bicycle.
BOB:	I remember.
SHEILA:	I fancied one of the full-backs.
KENNY:	And she ended up marrying him.
BOB:	Right then. Here's to the Walkergate Dynamos.

(They raise their glasses and drink the toast.)

ALL:	The Walkergate Dynamos.

(BOB gets up from the table and crosses to address the audience.)

BOB: Let's not bother about what we ate.
              Basically it was fast food served very slowly,
              and not a patch on Doyle's at Sydney
              Harbour.

              *(Beyond him, the WAITER arrives at the
              table with a trolley laden with bottles. He
              pours from a variety of bottles into a
              variety of glasses, more or less matching
              BOB'S commentary.)*

BOB: We had an amusing little Chardonnay with
              the fish. And with the meat a very rare Nuit
              St Georges specially guaranteed not to
              impair the delicate flavour of the mashed
              taties. We had a sweet Muscat to go with
              the ethnic bread-and-butter pudding. Then
              brandy and port to go with the coffee, cigars
              and After-Eights. Oh yes, and Ralph had a
              couple of halves of spa water. Alcohol free,
              'cause he was driving.

              *(BOB returns to the table, which is a mass
              of bottles and glasses. KENNY is smoking a
              large cigar.)*

KENNY: So what do you think, Bob?
BOB: About what?
KENNY: About this place? The food? The drink? The
              ambience?
BOB: It's not bad.
KENNY: Not bad! Jesus wept! I bet you're going to
              tell me places like this are ten a penny in
              Australia.
BOB: Places like this are ten a penny in Australia.
KENNY: What? With sawdust on the floor and
              tarantula spiders in the soup.

BOB: Not in the soup. You order spiders as a side
              dish And they're not tarantulas. Redbacks
              and funnelwebs.
MARY: Take no notice of him, Kenny. Thank you
              for a lovely meal.

              (She nudges RALPH.)
RALPH: Yes. Thank you for a lovely meal. I enjoyed
              it all, especially the...

              (He tries to remember what he enjoyed best.)

BOB: The chips?
RALPH: The ambience.
SHEILA: It's the speciality of the house.
BOB: What did it used to be, this place? It's a
              conversion, isn't it?
SHEILA: It used to be a church.
BOB: Ah. Ye cannot serve God and Mammon.
KENNY: Well you're never going to make any money
              running a place like this as a church, are
              you?
BOB: Obviously. It wouldn't be commercially
              viable.
KENNY: We kept the font. Made it into a featurette.
MARY: I thought it looked like a font.
KENNY: That's because it's a font. Some silly sod put
              a preservation order on it.
RALPH: The Gospel according to St Matthew.
BOB: How's that again?
KENNY: St Matthew? Know the name. Can't put a
              face to it.
RALPH: The Gospel according to St Matthew. Ye
              cannot serve God and Mammon.
KENNY: And the lad was right. You can't serve both.
              So me, I signed on the dotted line for
              Mammon PLC.

BOB:	I think I might have just guessed that, comrade.
KENNY:	And we collect money in the font. For charity like. We send old people to Skegness.
BOB:	Lucky them. What comes next? The O.B.E.? Or is it straight for the knighthood?
MARY:	Stop being such a misery, our Bob.
BOB:	Sorry. I just wish the workmanship was a bit better, that's all.
KENNY:	The what?

(He hasn't heard the word in years.)

BOB:	The workmanship.
KENNY:	What's the matter with the workmanship?
BOB:	What's the matter with it? There isn't any.

(Maybe he gets up and points out the bits as he talks about them. We don't need to see them, of course. Do it with acting.)

| BOB: | These imitation plastic walnut panels. They're all coming adrift. And these shelves, they're out of true. And look at those joints. Can't you find any decent joiners any more? Do they not serve apprenticeships? |

KENNY:	Apprenticeships? That's ancient history, man. Bobby. We don't have apprenticeships. We have schemes.
BOB:	This isn't proper building work. It's Lego land. And I'll tell you something else. Underneath all this ticky-tacky, there's a church that was built to last, by proper craftsmen.
KENNY:	So?

BOB:	So that doesn't look like progress to me.
KENNY:	I don't need progress. I don't need things built to last. I want things built quickly by a bunch of cowboys on bonus. Another year, I'll have got rid of this place anyway...
BOB:	You'll have got rid of it?
KENNY:	Certainly I will. As a going concern. I've got six offers on the desk even as we speak. Four Mister Patels and two Mr Wongs.

(BOB gives up on the debate and returns to the table. He pours himself a brandy.)

KENNY:	It's a gravy train.
BOB:	No it isn't. It's a balloon. Full of hot air.
KENNY:	All right, so it's a balloon. And balloons burst. You just have to make sure somebody else is holding the piece of string when the balloon bursts.
BOB:	The Gospel according to PLC.
KENNY:	And the sanity clause is...who's holding the string?
BOB:	I give up.
	(He looks at the others.)
BOB:	What do you all think? Am I the only one in step?
SHEILA:	I don't think. I'm only the woman.
BOB:	Mary?
MARY:	I still think you're a misery.
BOB:	Ralph?
KENNY:	This should be good.
RALPH:	I want to know what you think about amateurs.
BOB:	Amateurs? Ask Kenny. He employed a bunch of amateurs to build this place for him.

RALPH:	Not builders. Footballers. Bishop Auckland, to be precise.
KENNY:	That's very precise but what are you talking about?
RALPH:	Bob Hardisty.
BOB:	*(Smiles)* I know what he's talking about.
SHEILA:	You're the only one in step. Again.
RALPH:	Bob Hardisty, captain of the Bishop Auckland team that dominated amateur football during the 1950's.
KENNY:	What about him?
BOB:	He was bald.
MARY:	Of course.
	(She understands.)
SHEILA:	Of course.
	(She doesn't.)
KENNY:	I blame that mineral water. It addles the brain.
	(He checks the bottle.)
MARY:	It's very simple. It's dreamtime.
KENNY:	That explains everything.
BOB:	We'll have him in the squad.
RALPH:	I think he's worth it. I saw him play.
BOB:	Me too. At St James's.
RALPH:	Cup Final replay.
BOB:	Against Crook Town.
RALPH:	That's the one.
BOB:	Good match an' all.

(Against this exchange, KENNY'S mobile telephone rings.)

BOB:	Your canary wants a word with you.

(KENNY brings his telephone from his pocket. He extends the aerial and speaks into it.)

KENNY:	*(On phone)* Yes...what's the problem? Right...I'll be there in ten minutes. *(Puts the phone away again. Turns to the others.)*
KENNY:	Sorry folks. Business calls.
SHEILA:	What's her name?
KENNY:	Don't be like that, pet.
SHEILA:	Apologies. What is the nature of your business problem?
KENNY:	Bit of a fight at Wor Jacky's.
BOB:	Wor Jacky's?
KENNY:	Little place I've got near the Bigg Market.
BOB:	What is it?
KENNY:	Wine bar and disco.
BOB:	And you called it after Jacky Milburn?
KENNY:	Thing about wine bars and discos, they've got to have a theme that'll capture the imagination of the punters. What better way to celebrate our greatest hero?
BOB:	Little kids getting pissed out of their minds and kicking each other's heads in? I can think of a thousand better ways.
KENNY:	Just another first-class carriage on the gravy train.
BOB:	Or another balloon?
KENNY:	No time to argue the toss. Duty calls. *(He gets up. Turns to SHEILA.)*
KENNY:	I might be late. Ask Bobby nicely, he'll probably see you home. *(He turns to the others.)*
KENNY:	Thank you for the pleasure of your company. If you've enjoyed this place, tell your friends. If you haven't, keep your bloody mouth shut. *(Turns to band.)*
KENNY:	Bit of live music for the boss, lads.

(*As KENNY exits, the band plays a suitable fragment: say a boppish paraphrase of the HALLELUJAH CHORUS. Reactions from the others. A bit of shuffling then:*)

RALPH: Nobby Stiles went bald, didn't he?
(*Lighting change.*
BOB steps forward to address audience.
Music does a seamless segue into SHEILA'S theme.)

BOB: I took Sheila home in a taxi. We put the fare on Kenny's account. That way Bede Investments PLC could claim it against tax. They had this big house in Jesmond. In fact, it filled most of Jesmond and overlapped into Gosforth.

(*BOB walks across into SHEILA'S living room - indicated by a long, plush, semi-circular settee or such, plus optional rug. There's a strong smell of money about the place.*
SHEILA sits at one end of the settee.
BOB takes in the scene.)

BOB: So this is home?
SHEILA: One of them.
BOB: How many more have you got?
SHEILA: A little place in the country, a flat in London, a time-share in Spain. They're not exactly homes. They're mostly tax losses for Bede Investments.
BOB: And have you found true happiness?
SHEILA: Next question.
BOB: When Kenny got his phone call...you said: what's her name?

77

SHEILA:	Yes.
BOB:	Does he have other women?
SHEILA:	Yes.
BOB:	Do you mind?
SHEILA:	I'm past caring.
BOB:	Nobody's ever past caring.
SHEILA:	Well...
	(A shrug.)
	Serves me right for watching the Walkergate Dynamos.
BOB:	And fancying the full-back.
SHEILA:	The wages of fancying full-backs.
BOB:	I have another question.
SHEILA:	I dare you to ask it.

(Pause.)

BOB:	Which one did you really fancy?
SHEILA:	I fancied you, bonny lad.
BOB:	That's what Kenny said.
SHEILA:	When did he say that?
BOB:	Thirty years ago.
SHEILA:	You didn't do much about it.
BOB:	Yes I did.
SHEILA:	Not so's anybody would notice.
BOB:	I'll tell you what happened. I was working on a building site with Kenny. It was my last week at work.

(He crosses to building site: more or less imaginary. Maybe BOB and KENNY don caps.)

KENNY:	You'll miss all this in Australia, comrade.
BOB:	All what?
KENNY:	The cold. The wet. The lousy wages. The exploitation.

BOB:	Why do you think I'm going?
KENNY:	Are you going to take Sheila out before you go?
BOB:	Sheila who?
KENNY:	Oh howay man. The little lass that watches us playing football.
BOB:	Why should I?
KENNY:	'Cause she fancies you.
BOB:	What's the odds? I'm leaving the country.
KENNY:	Give her something to remember you by. And if anything goes wrong, you'll be the other side of the world in Wagga Wagga so what's the odds?
BOB:	*(To SHEILA)* I didn't really know what he was on about. I was dead innocent in them days.
SHEILA:	You haven't changed.
BOB:	*(To KENNY)* I don't even know how to get in touch with her.
KENNY:	You use the miracle of the electric telephone.
BOB:	Is she on the phone?
KENNY:	She works on the switchboard at the biscuit factory.
BOB:	How do you know that?
KENNY:	I make it my business to know things. I'll be famous for it one day.

(BOB returns to the living room and the present. KENNY exits.)

BOB:	So I telephoned the biscuit factory. *(Picks up telephone.)* Is that Sheila? *(Across the stage, a pool of light on LIZ, a Geordie lass, and hint of an old-style telephone switchboard. Headphones will do.)*

LIZ:	No.
BOB:	Is she there?
LIZ:	Who wants her?
BOB:	I do.
LIZ:	Who are you when you're at home?
BOB:	The name's Bob.
LIZ:	What firm do you represent?
BOB:	I don't represent a firm. I'm my own man. I represent myself. And the workers of the world.
LIZ:	Eee, you fancy yourself, don't you?
BOB:	Look. I just want to speak to Sheila.
LIZ:	She isn't here. She's having her dinner.
BOB:	Will you give her a message?
LIZ:	Is it personal?
BOB:	Of course it's personal.
LIZ:	We're not allowed personal phone calls. Only official representatives of accredited firms.
BOB:	I eat your bloody biscuits. What more do you want?
LIZ:	There's no need for that sort of talk.
BOB:	It's really personal...and really intimate... *(He makes it sound highly sexy. He turns to SHEILA.)* That made her take notice.
SHEILA:	It would. I remember Lizzie Armstrong. Cheeky little cow.
	(BOB resumes phone call.)
BOB:	Listen. Write this down. It's a message from Bob the full-back. I am going to Australia on Thursday to start a new life. Will you meet me on Wednesday night? I'll be outside the Oxford Galleries at half-past eight.
LIZ:	*(Lagging well behind)* A message from Bob

	the full-back. I am going to...where?
BOB:	Australia!
LIZ:	Is that A.U.S?
BOB:	Never mind where I'm going
LIZ:	I'm just a telephonist. I don't do shorthand.
BOB:	Oxford Galleries, Wednesday, half-past eight. That's all she needs to know.
LIZ:	Oxford Galleries...
BOB:	Get a shift on, I haven't got any more pennies.

(The line goes dead. Lights out on LIZ. Back to the present.)

BOB:	Did you ever get the message?
SHEILA:	Oh yes. I got the message.
BOB:	And you realise I had overlooked one vital factor?
SHEILA:	Which was?
BOB:	Newcastle United had a home game on the Wednesday night.
SHEILA:	I realised it next day when I read the Chronicle. They beat Fulham 7-2.
BOB:	Two goals each by Gilfillon, Neal and Tuohy, and one by Len White.
SHEILA:	I'm not interested in who scored the goals.
BOB:	I suppose not.
SHEILA:	But I'm glad they won. It would have been terrible if you'd stood me up and then lost the match.
BOB:	That wasn't the end of it.
SHEILA:	No?
BOB:	No. After the game, I ran all the way to the Oxford to see if you were there. I got there about half-past nine but of course, you weren't there.
SHEILA:	Hardly surprising in the circumstances.

BOB:	I'm sorry.
SHEILA:	I know my place. If the lads have a home game...
BOB:	It's not that simple.
SHEILA:	I'm only the woman.
BOB:	I'm standing outside the Oxford. You're not there. What do you think I did then?
SHEILA:	The same as any self-respecting macho Geordie. You went into the nearest pub and got blind drunk.
BOB:	No.
SHEILA:	No?
BOB:	I walked down to the Quayside.

(Lighting change.
We see BOB'S memory of the Quayside
and the Bridge, and also SHEILA in the
living room.
BOB moves halfway between the two,
between past and present.)

BOB: I sat on a bollard under the Tyne Bridge. I could hear music. Some guy playing Body and Soul on a tenor sax.

(Band plays the music.)

BOB: It must have been coming from a pub or wasn't there a jazz club in the Royal Arcade? Well, wherever it was coming from, that's what I heard. And I sat there, looked at the water and I cried my eyes out.

SHEILA: Were you crying for me?

BOB: It was all sorts of things, all mixed up. I'd promised my Dad I'd look after my mother and here I was, getting the Hell out. Maybe I was crying in case I never saw United play again. Could have been I was crying for the Tyneside I was leaving behind. Or for what might happen to Tyneside when I wasn't there to keep an eye on things.

(A beat then:)

BOB:	And I might have been crying for you.
SHEILA:	At least I was in the frame. Outsider. Slightly fancied. Worth a small each-way bet.
BOB:	More than that.
SHEILA:	Getaway. You cleared off to Australia and forgot all about me.
BOB:	I thought I'd forgotten.

(Lighting change. Lose the Bridge.
BOB returns to the living room.
Music gently fades.)

BOB:	I fell in love with Australia. The bridges are bigger and you can breathe deeply and it doesn't make you cough. I took out naturalisation papers. Swore an oath of allegiance to the Queen and became an Australian.
SHEILA:	An old socialist like you? An oath of allegiance to the Queen?
BOB:	I kept my fingers crossed.
SHEILA:	And you got married?
BOB:	Don't we all?
SHEILA:	Yes, we do, don't we?
BOB:	Had kids, worked hard, joined the union, dived into the deep end of the Australian Labour Party.
SHEILA:	Is it like the British Labour Party?
BOB:	Very similar. We spend more time fighting

with each other than we do fighting the
enemy. A very wise drunken friend in
Sydney once said...the Australian Labour
Party...they remember the words but they've
forgotten the tune.

(Then a sudden change of tack.)

Does the date November the 11th mean
anything to you?

SHEILA: Armistice Day. We used to have two
minutes' silence, didn't we? The traffic
would stop.

BOB: And we'd remember people like my Dad.

SHEILA: We don't do it any more.

BOB: Why waste two minutes on silence, when
you could be making money?

SHEILA: I don't remember it stopping. Just, suddenly,
it wasn't there any more. Suppose it got run
over by the gravy train.

BOB: Like everything else.

SHEILA: Well that's the answer. Armistice Day. Ask
me another.

BOB: What else happened on November the 11th?

SHEILA: No idea. I'm hopeless at Trivial Pursuits.

BOB: It's the day the British hanged Ned Kelly.

SHEILA: Ned Kelly. He was a sort of highwayman,
wasn't he?

BOB: Not to us. A freedom fighter. He said up
yours to the Brits. We like anybody who
does that.

SHEILA: Armistice Day and Ned Kelly. I'll try to
remember in future.

BOB: Armistice Day, Ned Kelly and Gough
Whitlam.

SHEILA: Gough Whitlam? He was your Prime
Minister, right?

BOB: Right.

SHEILA: Did the British hang him as well?

BOB:	More or less.
SHEILA:	I don't remember that.
	(Lighting change.
	Again we see the Bridge, but now it's
	Sydney Harbour with the Opera House in
	the background.
	Again BOB moves halfway between the two
	spaces and the two time scales.
	Music: a fragment of WALTZING MATILDA.)
BOB:	I don't suppose you realise what Gough
	Whitlam did for Australia.
SHEILA:	Sorry, pet. No idea. I'm only the woman.
BOB:	He made us into Australians. Instead of
	plastic Englishmen. We got our very own
	National Anthem. We got rid of...
	(Music: a fragment of GOD SAVE THE
	QUEEN.)
	...and replaced it with Australia Fair.
	(Music: fragment of AUSTRALIA FAIR.)
	Musically they're both terrible but the
	principle's a good one. Do you realise, up
	until Comrade Whitlam came along, kids
	were only taught English history in schools?
	English Kings and Queens and Prime
	Ministers? We got rid of that as well. Got to
	grips with our own history.
SHEILA:	Rolf Harris? Germaine Greer? Dame Edna?
BOB:	It's a bigger history than that.
SHEILA:	Dreamtime.
BOB:	You know about dreamtime?
SHEILA:	I read books.
BOB:	Our history's a dreamtime of serpents and
	red rock and Aboriginal people who
	remember the tune, even if the white man
	took away their words.
SHEILA:	That's the hard bit. Remembering the tune.

BOB:	But we made one fatal mistake, me and my good friend, Comrade Whitlam. You can change your National Anthem and you'll get away with it. You can change your history and get away with it. But don't upset your American friends.
SHEILA:	Isn't that what friends are for?
BOB:	See, it's a big country. Imagine all this is Australia.

(He indicates the entire stage area. Then picks on a spot in the middle.)

BOB:	Right in the middle, where you only find serpents and red rock, the Americans had military bases. Because of the military threat from South-East Asia. All part of the plan to stop North Vietnam invading San Francisco. So Gough Whitlam said this is a load of bollocks. Hadaway back to your own country.
SHEILA:	Yanks go home.
BOB:	Exactly. As it turns out, it wasn't a smart thing to say. The White House said to Whitehall, it's your Commonwealth. Get rid of this turbulent priest. And since the British government crawls to the Americans faster than anybody in the world, they did as they were told.
SHEILA:	On November the 11th?
BOB:	November the 11th, 1975, Gough Whitlam was pushed out of office by the British Government. They used Clause Four, chapter seven, verse nine, sub-section thirty-one of the Magna Carta or some such crap. Basically, they stitched him up.
SHEILA:	Why didn't you fight?
BOB:	We were close to it. Australia was a cough and spit away from civil war. There were

	people on our side with guns. And people on their side with bigger guns.
SHEILA:	Maybe they only look bigger.
BOB:	Maybe so. But we didn't fight. And I bet you can guess what I did. I went down to the harbour, sat down under the bridge, looked at the black water...
SHEILA:	And cried your eyes out?
BOB:	Yes.

(He sits down, still halfway between past and present.)

BOB:	This time there was no music. Just a terrible silence. We'd tried to build a great bridge and we'd almost done it when these time-servers came along from Whitehall and kicked it to bits with their shiny shoes.

(He covers his head with his hands.)

SHEILA:	Is it worth crying about politics?

(BOB lowers his hands and looks at her.)

BOB:	I wasn't crying about politics. I was crying about poor, pathetic little Bobby Rutherford from Byker. My mother had just died and I hadn't gone back for the funeral because I was too busy with the revolution. And my marriage was breaking up. I'd been unfaithful to my wife.
SHEILA:	You? I don't believe that.
BOB:	Not with other women. Only with the Labour movement.
SHEILA:	Behind every great man there's a little woman saying: where the Hell have you been till this time?
BOB:	You know about that?

SHEILA:	The wit and wisdom of Kenny Turnbull PLC.
BOB:	So I sat there in the darkness, and I tried to talk to my Dad.

(He calls into the darkness.)

BOB:	Dad? Are you there? I've buggered things up, and I need your help, 'cause I don't know what to do.

(Turns to SHEILA.)

And do you know who I saw?

SHEILA:	Ned Kelly?
BOB:	No. Not Ned Kelly. Not my Dad either.

(He turns again to look into the darkness. A light in the darkness, but he doesn't see his father. Instead, the same image as in Act One: SHEILA, in her late teens, leaning on a bicycle. She wears a raincoat and red beret perched on the side of her head - a little bit saucy like.)

BOB:	Sheila!

(She raises her hand in a discreet wave. BOB waves back.
Lighting change.
Lose the Bridge and the Harbour and we're back in the living room and the present.)

BOB:	I saw you. With your bicycle and your little red hat. The same way I used to see you on the touchline when I was playing for the Walkergate Dynamos.
SHEILA:	Thank you for the compliment.
BOB:	It was like you were sending me a message. Across the world and across the years.
SHEILA:	*(Suggests)* Howay the lads?

(BOB smiles.)

BOB:	It all sounds daft when I tell it.
SHEILA:	Daft things are best.
BOB:	Anyway. I'm sorry. I apologise.
SHEILA:	What for?
BOB:	Standing you up, outside the Oxford Galleries.
SHEILA:	It wasn't a problem.
BOB:	It wasn't?
SHEILA:	No.

(Sudden thought strikes BOB.)

BOB:	Hey! Did *you* turn up?
SHEILA:	What do you think?
BOB:	I mean, if you stood me up as well, it could mean civil war.
SHEILA:	Yes, I turned up. I wasn't all that optimistic, because I knew there was a match on. I waited ten minutes.
BOB:	Only ten minutes?
SHEILA:	Call it fifteen.
BOB:	That's better.
SHEILA:	Then I went to the pictures.
BOB:	I see.
	(Pause.)
BOB:	What did you go to see?
SHEILA:	South Pacific.
BOB:	Any good?
SHEILA:	Not bad.
BOB:	Is that the one where Debbie Reynolds washes her hair?
SHEILA:	That's the one. I bet you're good at Trivial Pursuits.
BOB:	Red hot. As long as they're really trivial. It's Important Pursuits where the trouble starts.

(He looks at his watch. Gets up.)
Time I was going. There'll be Hell to pay if
Ralphy's made the cocoa and it's getting
cold.

SHEILA: I'll ring for a taxi.

BOB: There's no need.

SHEILA: It'll go on the account.

BOB: I fancy the walk.

SHEILA: Down to the river?

BOB: Maybes.

SHEILA: Suit yourself, bonny lad.

*(They look at each other. No physical
contact. Then a sharp breakaway.
SHEILA exits. BOB steps forward to address
the audience.
Music starts: a sharp, edgy percussion.
Note: whenever BOB is out of doors, he
wears an Oz-style bush hat: sort of modified
Mick Dundee style.)*

BOB: I walked into the city centre. I managed to
dodge most of the motorways. I found
myself in the Bigg Market.

*(Flashing blue lights. Police sirens. Sound
of breaking glass. Shouts.
Music echoes the scene: free-form blowing:
Coltrane sheets of sound?)*

BOB: Apparently it was just another Saturday
night. The finest flowers of Geordie youth
peeing and puking all over estate agents'
windows. Those who could still stand
were kicking lumps out of each other. There
was a fire engine outside Wor Jacky's wine
bar. Nobody was singing folk songs.

*(Chants of 'Here we go, here we go, etc.'
Two LADS approach BOB, one either side
of him. They are full of drunken menace.)*

1ST LAD: Eee lad, where did you get that hat?

(BOB goes into a broad Australian accent.)

BOB: Australia, mate.
2ND LAD: Are you from Australia?
BOB: Too right.
1ST LAD: You're a long way from home.
BOB: That's why I wear a big hat.
2ND LAD: Do you know Paul Hogan?
BOB: No but I'm in the same business.
1ST LAD: Are you a comedian?
2ND LAD: We're not keen on comedians.
1ST LAD: They don't make us laugh.
BOB: I kill crocodiles.
1ST LAD: Getaway man.
BOB: I kill crocodiles for a living. Sharks for food.
            Pommie bastards for fun. Do you want to
            see my implement?

*(He reaches inside his jacket, as for a
knife.)*

1ST LAD: No thanks.
2ND LAD: No offence, pal.

(They move away into the darkness.)

BOB: *(Calls after them)* See you later, sports. *(To
            audience)* Sheila was right. I needed the
            river.

(The noise and flashing lights fade.

Music segues into a quiet, bluesy theme.
BOB sits down on a bollard beneath the
Bridge.)

BOB: I stared at the black water and...

                (He covers his head with his hands.
                He cries, but not so's anyone would notice.
                Except that we know.
                We gradually become aware of someone else
                sitting on the quayside. He's older than
                BOB, but sort of ageless. His name is
                HARRY. He wears a slightly battered tuxedo
                and has an instrument case with him: a
                tenor sax to be precise.
                Out of the silence:)

HARRY: I once played with Bing Crosby, you know.

                (BOB looks up, reacts:)

BOB: You what?
HARRY: And Sinatra.
BOB: Getaway.
HARRY: Weedy little guy, Sinatra. Thin.
BOB: So I believe.
HARRY: And Bing wore a wig. He was bald,
                underneath it.
BOB: Makes sense.

                (A beat then:)

BOB: I could maybe get him a game of football.
HARRY: He was a singer.
BOB: Sorry.

                (Each concludes the other is a nutter, but

harmless.)

BOB:	You a musician?
HARRY:	Done the lot.
BOB:	Is that right?
HARRY:	Theatres, dance-halls, ships' cruises.
BOB:	What do you play?
HARRY:	Played for them all, in the theatre. Pit orchestras, like. Laurel and Hardy. George Formby. Jimmy James.
BOB:	Jimmy James?
HARRY:	He did a drunk act.
BOB:	I know. I saw him.
HARRY:	But he was teetotal. Never touched a drop.
BOB:	Gambler, though, wasn't he? The horses?
HARRY:	Played at the Palace.
BOB:	A command performance?
HARRY:	In the Haymarket.
BOB:	Oh. That Palace. I wondered, see, 'cause I swore an oath of allegiance to the Queen...
HARRY:	Great orchestra, at the Palace.
BOB:	Was it?
HARRY:	Every one a drunk. Except the drummer.
BOB:	He was teetotal?
HARRY:	The drummer was deaf.
BOB:	Must have been a great orchestra.

(HARRY pauses, to listen to the sound of a police siren.)

HARRY:	Listen.
BOB:	Police car. The country's going to Hell.
HARRY:	That's a C natural and an E flat, repeating. *(M.D. to advise on the accuracy of his ears.)*

BOB:	I see. It sounds like music to you.
HARRY:	Everything's music.
	(He listens again as the sound fades.)

HARRY:	Not much of a tune.
BOB:	What have you got in your case? Tenor sax?
HARRY:	I play anything the people want. Theatres, dance-halls, ships' cruises, pantomimes, summer seasons.
BOB:	Jazz?
HARRY:	Tenor sax, doubling clarinet and violin, but that was only the summer seasons.
BOB:	Did you ever play jazz?
HARRY:	Tried. But it's hard.

(From hereabouts, the dialogue is punctuated by music - probably solo tenor, but that too is up to the M.D.)

BOB:	I know it's hard.
HARRY:*	Got the wrong colour skin, see?

(Holds up his hands for BOB to see.)

BOB:	There's been some great white jazz musicians.
HARRY:	Afro-American music, jazz.
BOB:	Bix Beiderbecke...
HARRY:	Louis Armstrong, Duke Ellington, Charlie Parker...
BOB:	Did you play with any of them?
HARRY:	I listened. That's all I did. Listened. And I thought: I've got the wrong colour skin. But still, I tried.
BOB:	You played jazz in Newcastle?
HARRY:	Everywhere. Played everywhere.
BOB:	Sydney? In Australia?
HARRY:	Everywhere. But, man, it's hard to play jazz.
BOB:	I think I might have heard you.
HARRY:	I don't have the rage, you see.
BOB:	The rage?

HARRY:	If you're black, there's a rage inside. There's bound to be, if you think about it. Slavery and such.
BOB:	Maintain the rage.
HARRY:	We don't have that. We have rage, but it's another sort of rage.
BOB:	Gough Whitlam said that to the Australian people. Whatever else you do...maintain the rage.

(Again there is the sound of a police siren. Again HARRY pauses to listen.)

BOB:	What's that one? The same?
HARRY:	A flat and a B natural.
BOB:	The police were never out of tune in the old days.
HARRY:	I heard Coleman Hawkins. In New York. When I was working the liners.
BOB:	You heard Hawk?
HARRY:	On 52nd Street.
BOB:	Hey, man, that must have been amazing.
HARRY:	His music droppeth like a gentle rage from Heaven, upon the place beneath. Thrice blessed. I was seriously tempted to pack it all in and get a proper job.
BOB:	But you didn't.
HARRY:	I've watched people with proper jobs. Audience people. Dancing people. Drinking people. They don't listen to the music. They don't listen to each other. They watch each other. Spotting the winners and the losers. Me. I never wanted to be a winner or a loser. Never wanted to be on the team. I don't play the game.
BOB:	Lucky man.
HARRY:	Do you play a game?

BOB:	I'm a joiner by trade.
HARRY:	See. What I do on the outside, matches what I am on the inside. I'll never be Coleman Hawkins, but at least I'm all in one piece.
BOB:	Yes. Me too. I love the smell of timber.
HARRY:	It's when the outside and the inside don't match up that you get trouble. Both sides hate each other so they take it out on the rest of the world. People hit each other. And responsible citizens send for the police.

(As they hear the sound of another police siren.)

BOB:	What key?
HARRY:	That's the first one back again. He's always busy on a Saturday night.

(BOB gets up and crosses to him.)

BOB:	Listen. I've got an important question to ask.
HARRY:	To be or not to be?
BOB:	Did you ever play jazz in Newcastle in August 1960?
HARRY:	It's possible.
BOB:	Or in Sydney a couple of months ago?
HARRY:	Also possible.
BOB:	Anything's possible, I suppose.
HARRY:	It's possible I'm crazy. Or you're crazy. Or we're both crazy.
BOB:	Try this for a possibility. Thirty years ago, I sat here, and I heard a tenor playing up there somewhere.. *(Points up the hill towards the town centre)* ...a guy playing Body and Soul.

HARRY:	Body and Soul?
	(An echo from the band.)
BOB:	Was it you playing that night?
	(HARRY shakes his head.)
HARRY:	Not possible.
BOB:	But you said you'd played jazz in Newcastle...
HARRY:	I never played that tune.
BOB:	It's a good tune.
HARRY:	I heard Coleman Hawkins play Body and Soul on 52nd Street in New York. What a piece of work. There was no point in me playing it after Hawk had played it. I know sacrilege when I hear it.
BOB:	I see.
	(Sits down, disappointed.)
BOB:	So it wasn't you?
HARRY:	Not me. Not possible. For the reason stated.
BOB:	Shame.
HARRY:	But if you heard it...
BOB:	I heard it, clear as a bell...
HARRY:	If you really heard it, it doesn't matter who was playing it. It doesn't matter if nobody was playing it. Hearing the music, that's all that matters.
	(Music builds. Lighting change. BOB steps forward to audience.)
BOB:	I flew back to Sydney a couple of weeks later. Mary and Ralph came to the airport with me.

	(MARY and RALPH enter.
	RALPH is pushing a luggage trolley, which
	he hands on to BOB.)
MARY:	Have you got everything you need?
BOB:	No. That would be greedy.
RALPH:	I have an announcement to make.
BOB:	You're not pregnant again?
RALPH:	Don't be daft, Bob, men don't get pregnant.
BOB:	*(To MARY)* See? Still disenfranchised.

(RALPH brings a piece of paper from his pocket.)

RALPH:	The selection committee has finalised the baldy-headed squad for the Inter-Galactic Cup.
BOB:	We finished at three o'clock this morning. We needed extra cocoa.
RALPH:	In goal, Bruce Grobbelaar, Liverpool and Zimbabwe.
BOB:	He's receding rather than bald, but I was very keen on the post-imperialist touch.
RALPH:	Right full-back, Don Howe, West Bromwich Albion and England.
BOB:	It's an old-fashioned team with proper full-backs.
MARY:	Just like the Walkergate Dynamos?
BOB:	Oh, there'll never be a team like that one.
MARY:	Thank God for that.
RALPH:	Left full-back, playing out of position for the good of the side, Jim Iley of Newcastle United.
BOB:	You need good team spirit in the galaxy.
MARY:	So I'm told.
RALPH:	Right half-back, Bob Hardisty of Bishop Auckland and England.
BOB:	An amateur and a gentleman.

RALPH:	Centre-half. Jack Charlton of Ashington, Leeds United and England.
BOB:	A professional and as much of a gentleman as you could be, playing for Leeds United.
RALPH:	Left half-back, also playing out of position, Nobby Stiles, Manchester United and England.
BOB:	Not only bald but toothless. A double threat.
RALPH:	On the right-wing, Ralph Coates, one of the famous Geordies from Burnley in Lancashire. Inside-right, Pop Robson, of Sunderland...
BOB:	...and Newcastle United.
RALPH:	He played for both, see?
MARY:	Yes. I understand.
BOB:	Proving that the great nations of Tyne and Wear can live together in peace and harmony, given goodwill on both sides.
MARY:	I'll believe it when I see it.
RALPH:	Centre-forward, Hughie Gallacher, Newcastle United and Scotland.
BOB:	Wee Hughie. Tragic and legendary.
RALPH:	Inside-left, Keith Kettleborough, also of Newcastle United.
BOB:	Not exactly legendary but Ralph remembered him. Heroes must be honoured, even the anonymous ones.
RALPH:	And on the left-wing, but with a licence to roam, the great Bobby Charlton of Ashington, Manchester United, England and the World.
BOB:	Reserves to travel. Jimmy James...
RALPH:	Because Bob says every great football team needs a comedian.
BOB:	And Vladimir Ilyich Ulyanov Lenin.
RALPH:	I'm still not sure about Lenin.
MARY:	You can't have too many comedians.

BOB:	A football team is a collective enterprise. Individual genius serving the common good.
MARY:	Oh man, hadaway back to Australia.
BOB:	Right. I will.

(An incoherent flight announcement over.
BOB gives MARY a hug.)

BOB:	Look after your man. He's got a head full of dreams.
MARY:	Why do you think I married him?
BOB:	*(To RALPH)* See you later, sport.
RALPH:	Are you coming back?
BOB:	I doubt it.

(The whine of a jet. BOB and MARY exit.
Lighting change.
BOB wheels the luggage trolley off.
Music link: reprise of FLYING HOME.
BOB returns. He's now in the lee of the
Sydney Harbour Bridge with the Opera
House beyond.
It's a sunny day: a bobby-dazzler.)

BOB: So I went back. Bob Rutherford of Byker,
Walkergate Dynamos, Australia and the
World. It was good to be home.
I kept thinking: what's the difference
between little bridges and big bridges? And I
remembered when my Uncle George kept
goldfish, and he told me if you took a
goldfish from a bowl and put it in a pond, it
would grow bigger.
And because I'm a funny feller, that
reminded me of the World Cup and how we
all got excited about Gazza and Chrissie
Waddle and Peter Beardsley. And I thought:

here's three bonny lads that used to play for
United, but they don't play for United any
more. Why's that? Have they all signed on
the dotted line for Mammon PLC? Or was
the goldfish bowl too small for them?
And maybe that's the reason those lads
wanted to beat me up in the Bigg Market.
Because the goldfish bowl's too small.
Or is it that their inside doesn't match their
outside? Or they've never sat on a bench in
the back yard and listened to stories? Or
they can't hear any music? Maybe they
don't know there's music to be heard
anywhere.
I'll tell you one thing I found out. Sitting on
the quayside, looking at the waters of Tyne,
it reminds me that the river flows into the
North Sea, and that reminds me that
England is a small island.
Sitting on the harbour side, looking at the
white water, reminds me that it flows out
across the Great Barrier Reef into the Pacific
and then wraps itself around South-East
Asia and beyond.
Newcastle quayside tells you that you're
living on an island.
Sydney Harbour tells you that you're living
on a planet called the good earth.
But for God's sake, it's all the same water!
(SHEILA enters. She's dressed casually for
the weather, plus a little red hat, worn a
little bit saucy like...)

SHEILA: There's no need to shout.
BOB: Sorry. But I have to maintain the rage.

(She crosses to him.
They share the view.)

BOB:	Do you like it?
SHEILA:	It's big.
BOB:	There's no bigger sky anywhere in the world.

(A beat then:)

BOB:	Happy ending?
SHEILA:	It's a beginning.
BOB:	Happy beginning?
SHEILA:	We're in the frame. Good each-way bet.
BOB:	It's a good place to make bridges.

(A little music gently fading in.
BODY AND SOUL.)

SHEILA:	There's something you're forgetting.
BOB:	What?
SHEILA:	You owe me a dance.
BOB:	I stood you up, didn't I? Tell you what. We'll get a boat and I'll show you the real South Pacific.
SHEILA:	You still owe me a dance.
BOB:	There's no music.
SHEILA:	I can hear music.

(BOB listens.)

BOB:	In that case, so can I. May I have this dance?
SHEILA:	You may.

(They assume dancing position, a little self-conscious and awkward.)

BOB:	Welcome home.

(They freeze.
Music builds.
Fade to BLACKOUT.)

THE END